ADVENTURES

M*in*BILE

HOMES

HOW I GOT STARTED IN MOBILE HOME INVESTING AND HOW YOU CAN TOO!

RACHEL HERNANDEZ

Library of Congress Control Number: 2011916540

ISBN (13): 978-0-9839492-0-6
ISBN (10): 0-9839492-0-4

Published by:
Bitter Melon Publishing LLC
San Antonio, Texas
Web: bittermelonpublishing.com

Printed in the United States of America

Version 1.0

Book Design by Darlene Swanson of www.van-garde.com

Dedication

This book is dedicated to all those
who have helped me through the years.

I could not have done it without you.

Thank you for believing in me.

LEGAL DISCLAIMER

This publication is designed to provide reliable and competent information regarding the subject matter covered. It is sold with the understanding that the publisher and the author are not engaged in rendering legal, accounting or other professional advice. Laws and practices often differ from state to state and country to country. If legal advice or other expert assistance is required, the services of a competent professional should be sought.

It is not the purpose of this book to reprint all of the information that is otherwise available to those interested in mobile home investing, but instead to complement, amplify and supplement other related texts. The reader is urged to read all available material, learn as much as possible about mobile home investing and cater the information to his or her individual needs before beginning to invest in mobile homes. For more information, see the recommended resources in Appendix 2.

Every effort has been made to make this book as complete and accurate as possible. However, there may be mistakes, both typographical and in content. This book should only be used as a general guide and not the ultimate source of mobile home investing information. Furthermore, this book contains information on mobile home investing that is current only up to the printing date.

The purpose of this book is to educate and entertain. The publisher and the author shall have neither liability nor responsibility to any person or entity with respect to any loss or damage caused, or alleged to have been caused, directly or indirectly, by the information contained in this book.

Table of Contents

Introduction

Who Is This Book For?

This book is meant to serve as a companion book to other mobile home investing books available. It is meant as a supplement to the system of buying, selling and financing/lease optioning used mobile homes located in mobile home parks.

The purpose of this book is to inspire those interested in investing in mobile homes to get started and to get them through their first couple of deals. Here I share with you stories and adventures in mobile home investing based on my own experiences—the obstacles, the struggles and eventually the triumphs. If you have not read any books on mobile home investing, see the "Recommended Resources" section at the end of this book for a list of books I highly recommend.

Background

Like most real estate investors, I started out investing in single family homes. In the beginning, I found deals for other investors. After awhile, I started doing deals myself.

Soon I found myself always working and quickly burned out on being a landlord. So I dove into the wacky world of mobile home investing and here I am. It's much more fun. With mobile home investing, I have time to do things that I enjoy. I can work as much or as little as I want. I'm able to stop and start when I please. As a landlord, what I lacked was time—time to do the things I wanted to do, not just the things I had to do. With mobile home investing, I have the best of both worlds: I have time for myself, but still make enough money, and without the hassles of being a landlord.

Throughout my real estate investing career, I've attended a number of seminars. Each seminar taught me something new. After awhile, I must have attended every seminar out there on every possible subject on how to purchase real estate. I must have purchased over a couple dozen courses. My bookshelf was getting pretty crowded. One of those courses was Lonnie Scruggs' *Deals on Wheels* (back then it was a manual), which teaches about mobile home investing. It sat on my bookshelf for five years before I ever did anything serious with it. When I did, it changed my life. This is my story.

Chapter 1

My First Attempt at Mobile Home Investing

After I purchased Lonnie Scruggs' materials, I read not only them, but also read up all else I could on mobile home investing. I followed his course to the letter and found my first potential mobile home deal.

It was a two-bedroom, one-bath 1980s-style home in a family-style mobile home park. The sellers were moving and just needed to sell their home. They were asking $3,000 for the home. I met with the sellers and realized the home was in move-in-ready condition. I told them I'd buy the home just as long as it was OK with the park.

I went in to see the park manager and told her that I was thinking of buying and reselling the home. She told me she was sorry, but they did not allow anyone to purchase a home in their park who would not be living in the home. If I wanted to purchase the home, I'd have to move the home out of the park first, since I had no intention of living in the park.

I did some checking around and got some opinions

from other mobile home investors. I needed to see what other options were available. One investor in my area told me to buy the home for $1,000 and I could move it to one of his parks, which was over two hours away.

Being new to the game, I went ahead and met back up with the sellers. I told them the news and said the best I could do was purchase their home for $1,000. They were shocked and told me they could never accept such a low offer, and asked me to please leave. I left, never to hear back from them again.

A week later, I went back to the park manager in the same park. She told me the owners of that particular home had left the home and stripped it, taking most everything from the home with them, including the skirting and aluminum siding! Again, I kindly asked the park manager if I could work in the park to buy, sell and finance used mobile homes. She again told me no, but was nice about it. Yet again, she said they just did not allow that, and those were the rules.

Why I Waited Five Years to Start Investing in Mobile Homes

After this experience, I really got turned off to mobile home investing—this experience really left a bad taste in my mouth. The same investor in my area who had given me the advice to offer $1,000 for the mobile home encouraged me to help him work his parks two hours away. At the time, there were a lot of mobile home repossessions (bank owned) and opportunities that he just could not handle alone. Even back then, the competition among mobile home investors was minimal.

Because of my bad experience with the one particular park and the fact that this investor's parks were so far away, I declined his offer. I told him I'd just stick to single family homes. At the time, it just did not seem to me like it was worth it. After a few months, this investor was cash flowing beyond his wildest dreams with his mobile home investments. All along, I continued to pursue being a landlord and ended up getting burned out. Lonnie Scruggs' course, *Deals on Wheels*, sat on my bookshelf for five years before I did anything serious with it.

Early Beginnings

Five years later, I was a burned-out landlord constantly dealing with the hassles of landlording. I was in the middle of an eviction that took eight months and involved going through the court system. Dealing with the court system can be a very laborious and drawn-out process. I had gone through this process before, and was not looking forward to doing it again.

I brought in a professional property management company to help me with the eviction case. They hired an eviction company. I had been trying to work with these tenants for eight months while they kept stringing me along.

Finally, I decided enough was enough and we just needed to get this eviction done. My property manager called me on the day of the eviction. He told me the renters wanted to make payment arrangements for the past-due rent. I told him no arrangements, I just wanted to get this over and done with. So the eviction continued. Having to deal with this situation was draining the life out of me, both mentally and financially. Night after night, this eviction was on my mind. I could not sleep, and was having trouble functioning without first getting this situation taken care of. Having the eviction drag on due to the laborious court system only made things worse. Afterward, I made the decision that I was through with landlording and decided to cash out on my entire real estate portfolio.

Chapter 2

The Course That Took Five Years to Change My Life

After I got off the phone with the property management company, I sat for awhile. I began to think about my future. For years, I had been studying and applying the concepts I learned in real estate investing.

Now, a burned-out landlord, where did my future lie? Was all the time and energy spent on real estate investing just a waste of time? Were the stories I heard true? Did real estate investing, as a way to generate passive income, really work? Or were the stories just fables? I was beginning to doubt my interest in real estate investing at all.

As I was pondering my future as a real estate investor, I turned my attention to my bookshelf. I looked at the countless real estate courses and books sitting on my shelf. Every subject you can think of on real estate investing was on that shelf.

I thought back to all the money and time spent on books, courses, seminars, real estate forums, etc. What was I thinking? Were my peers and family right? Should I have continued my studies to get a graduate degree and in turn find a high-paying job just like everyone else? Did I really flush my hard-earned education and exemplary work experience in the corporate world right down the drain? What was it all for?

Just as I was really beginning to regret my interest and energy spent in real estate investing, one course in particular stood out and caught my eye. It was a lime green–colored manual sitting behind a bigger real estate course in a binder. Eyeing the bright color, it sparked my curiosity—I could not read the title from my perspective, and no longer remembered what it was. So I took it out from behind the larger course. It was Lonnie Scruggs' course, *Deals on Wheels*. I dusted it off and began to read his course again.

A Lightbulb Comes On

This time, while I was reading, a lightbulb came on in my head. I finally got it.

Five years ago, I read the course and thought, "Hey, this is a great way to make passive income in real estate," but that's about it. This time around, I thought, "Hey, this is a great way to make passive income and achieve financial freedom and have time to do the things I want to do, not the things I have to do." Big difference.

Back then, I was reading the course with a different set of eyes—an inexperienced set of eyes. Though I received a stream of income (i.e., rent payments) as a landlord, I still had a job.

As a landlord, every month there would always be issues with tenants. There would always be something that needed to be fixed, something that needed to be attended to. This cost both time and money. And every year it seemed like my expenses would go up—maintenance costs, property taxes, etc.

It was the management of these properties that really made things difficult. I had no time to do anything—even after I brought in property management companies to deal with the management hassles. I thought they could help the hassles go away. I was wrong.

In fact, bringing in property managers only made the situation worse. I still had a job—I had to manage the managers. I had to teach and direct people on what I already knew. Every time I heard my phone ring, I would cringe, as I knew there was another problem.

To be honest, I did not imagine the amount of time and energy involved in owning and managing properties until I was a landlord myself. It wasn't until I'd had the experience of managing rental properties and dealing with tenants that I was really able to value what I experience today—time. The time to do the things that I want to do, not the things I have to do. Now, I truly understood the words "financial freedom." I understood the meaning of passive income and having money work for me, not the other way around. Mobile home investing is truly a passive income source; I receive payments every month, but do not have to deal with the hassles of being a landlord and the upkeep involved with owning properties. I understood the way homeowners think versus the way renters think. People are much more likely to take care of something they own than something they do not.

That same day that I picked Lonnie Scruggs' course back up, I reread the entire thing. It was about fifty pages long. I went through it slowly and carefully, and highlighted and marked it up as best I could.

Afterward, I decided to take the day off and get online to the real estate forums and read as much as I could about mobile home investing. I was on a mission—a mission to learn. And I was obsessed.

My Passion for Mobile Home Investing Ignites

After reading Lonnie Scruggs' course again, the first thing I did was read and print out every article Lonnie wrote on mobile home investing. Then I searched the Web for all the other articles I could find on the topic.

It was insane. I read day and night, night and day. I read till my eyes popped out of my head. I went on the real estate message boards online and interacted with mobile home investors. I asked questions, many questions. I read. I responded. I was obsessed with learning as much as I could about investing in mobile homes. What were the pros? What were the cons? Was it realistic? What were the successes of those who had been in it? What were the failures? I was a sponge. And this time, the information stuck.

I even contacted that old investor from five years earlier to see how things were. He told me he was doing great. I told him about my frustrations of being a landlord and how I should have taken him up on his offer to work with him years ago and pursue mobile home investing. Knowing what I now knew about the importance of financial freedom, I was now more motivated than ever to achieve it. Thanks to all the reading I'd done, I knew this was something I could achieve through mobile home investing. This time, I knew things would be different.

He then went on to tell me that it seemed so long ago that he had made me the offer of working with him, and he had no regrets in his choice to pursue mobile homes as an investment vehicle. Nowadays, he said, he had so much free time on his hands. He had more than enough financially and now had plenty of time to pursue other interests. He had put his time in, and he had achieved his dreams of financial freedom. For me, I was just beginning.

Chapter 3

How I Got Started

So, how did I get started? Well, like most new investors, I was really scared about starting out. I had not the faintest idea what to do—I had Lonnie Scruggs' blueprint, but I just did not know how to go about implementing the ideas I learned in his course. So I did what I do best: I learned by fire, trial and error.

Visiting Mobile Home Parks, the Second Time Around

I will never forget the encounter I had during my first attempt at mobile home investing with the park manager who did not allow me to work in that particular park to buy, sell and finance used mobile homes. From that experience alone, I knew that getting to know the parks and the park managers in the area was key to being successful in this business. Without first creating a relationship with the park manager, it's next to impossible to work in a particular park.

I visited a few parks in my area, introduced myself

to the park managers and just got to know my market. I was terrified. Every time I went into a new park manager's office, I still remember my heart beating so loudly. But I forced myself to go. I had to succeed; there was no room for failure. And I found that each time it got easier and easier. I had no script, no idea what I was going to say. I just went in there with a mission of trying to find out as much information as I could—to get to know the park as well as the business.

And guess what? It worked. Most of the park managers were very friendly, and it turned out that the park manager who hadn't allowed me to buy and sell mobile homes in which I wouldn't be living was the exception, not the rule. Out of the 200 mobile home parks I visited in my area, I was only denied once by a park manager who told me they would not allow me to buy and sell used mobile homes in their parks. Unfortunately, they only allowed rentals. But that was the only park that denied me.

Found Some Parks to Work With; Now What?

Well, so I got to know some of the park managers. I told them I'd been looking for homes to buy, and my intent was to sell these homes on owner financing or to lease option them out. They agreed to allow me to work in the park just as long as any prospects passed the managers' credit application process and met the criteria for the park. Basically, they were allowed to deny or approve anyone who applied for the home who wished to live in the park.

We agreed. I left them all my name and contact information. So naturally I assumed the phone would start ringing with leads—right? Wrong.

I was not quite sure what had happened. I thought everything had gone OK during my one visit, and that would be enough to generate leads. It wasn't. None of the park managers had called me; there were no leads coming in. What I eventually learned was that since I had not yet built up a strong relationship with the park managers, I couldn't expect them to refer leads to me. It was up to me, not them, to go out and find leads. It was only over a period of time in which these relationships grew stronger that I eventually started receiving leads of mobile home sellers (as well as potential buyers) from park managers on a regular basis.

Chapter 4

My First Mobile Home Deal

Despite my high hopes, it took me eight months to find my first mobile home deal. Thank goodness it was in a park that I had already visited, where the park manager had given me permission to work.

The sellers had called me after seeing one of my flyers. When they called, my mind suddenly went blank. I had no idea what questions to ask. All those hours of studying really did not help me when it came time to put theory to action. *Great*, I thought, *now what?*

Why Everything Went Out the Window When It Came Time to Talk to Sellers

Lucky for me, the sellers were eager to explain their situation. Since they did most of the talking, I focused on listening. I tried not to scramble to remember what I had read about mobile home investing. It was too late for that. I needed just to focus my attention on the sellers and the issue at hand.

As it turned out, the sellers were as nervous as I was.

They told me they wanted to sell their home because it was getting crowded and they needed to live in a bigger home. I asked the questions that came naturally to me as a buyer of any home, including the condition of the home and the location.

But when I asked about the price, the sellers were silent. They said they did not want to discuss the price over the phone. For that, they wanted to meet me in person.

To me, this raised a red flag. I remembered reading a real estate course (one of the many sitting on my bookshelf) that cautioned against meeting sellers who call and do not name an asking price. According to the course, sellers who are motivated and serious about selling will always name a price. Those who do not are just testing the market, wanting to know what your price will be.

Then again, sometimes advice given in a course or book is based on the experiences of the writer and may not apply to everyone. For instance, this course also advised not answering the phone when sellers call, and letting calls go to voice mail, saying that if the sellers were really serious about selling, they would leave a voice mail message. This is not an approach I would use. I realized this course may not necessarily apply to my situation.

So I had two options here. Decide to go out and see the home. Or deny seeing the home until the sellers named their price over the phone. Since I had already broken the rule about not answering the phone, I decided to go against what the course advised. I set up an appointment to see the home. I'm glad I did.

Inspecting My First Mobile Home Deal

It turned out the sellers had lived in the home for ten years. They were long-term homeowners. The home was a two-bedroom, one-bath, 14 x 70 single wide, 1980s-type mobile home in good condition. It even had central heat and air-conditioning.

When I first arrived at the home, I inspected it as if I were planning to live there. I tested out everything and went through my checklist of questions I had prepared the night before.

After inspecting and going through the home both inside and out, I sat down with the sellers in the living room. I asked the sellers, a husband and wife, what their time frame was and asked what they were thinking of selling the home for. Then I closed my mouth and waited for their response.

The sellers told me they wanted to sell within a month. They still needed to find a new place to live, but knew the general vicinity of where they wanted to live. Wanting a quick sale, the sellers told me they were thinking of selling the home for $5,000.

Being new to mobile home investing, my mind blanked out again. To be honest, I was so nervous I just didn't know what to do. Though I did have a good feeling that the price was about right, I felt the need to double-check my figures. I told them that I would have to think about it. The sellers asked me when we could meet and talk again. I said I'd meet with them again in two days. Then I left.

Researching My First Mobile Home Deal

During the next two days, I took the time to research the home. I contacted my local housing authority in charge of manufactured homes to verify the title, and discovered the home was free of liens and no taxes were owed. So far, so good.

Then I researched the tax records for the home. According to the tax records, I found the current assessed value of the home was in the $4,000 price range.

I asked my local housing authority what the process was for transferring title and ownership of the home. Basically, they told me there could not be any liens on the home and past that it was just a matter of paperwork. Great!

A Second Meeting with the Sellers

Two days after our first meeting, the sellers called me. They asked whether I had made a decision about buying the home. Again, I asked the sellers what the best cash price they could offer would be. This time, they told me $4,200 cash. Again, I told them I would think about it, and suggested maybe we just meet up again in a few days. We all agreed.

A few days later, we met again. I came prepared and I showed the sellers the assessed value of the home according to the tax records. Again, I asked the sellers what the best cash price they could sell the home for would be. After a bit of negotiating, we came to an agreed purchase price of $3,600 cash. I had the home under contract that day.

Closing My First Mobile Home Deal

Within a few weeks, the sellers had their new home picked out. We went to the local housing authority together. We did the paperwork for the title transfer and exchanged the funds. I had the home sold in two weeks. I found plenty of prospective buyers just by placing a sign in the yard. It went for $10,000. I received $1,000 down and $250 monthly payments for four and a half years. This was my first deal. And my most memorable.

Chapter 5

Starting Out

There's so much information out there about mobile home investing—so many books, so many courses—and it can be very overwhelming trying to figure out where to begin. There have been many folks who have asked me the age-old question, "So…how do I get started?" Because I've gotten this question so many times, I've decided to provide an outline here, step by step, based on my experience.

Step 1: First Things First—
Figure Out Your "Why"

When I first started out in real estate investing, my "why" was really about creating passive income. But I did not understand the concept and importance of "financial freedom" until after I became a landlord. As a landlord, something was missing—the freedom part: having the time to do the things I wanted to do, not the things I had to do.

Only after my experience as a landlord, I truly knew and valued the concept of time and the importance of having the time to do the things I wanted to do. I truly understood the meaning of "financial freedom." Figuring out my "why" really gave me the passion and the drive to pursue mobile home investing.

Before you start investing, you must first figure out your "why." Why it is that you are interested in mobile home investing? What is your end goal? A good question that I always pose to people who are trying to figure out what direction to move in their lives is this: "If you could do anything in life and money were no object, what would you be doing?"

Don't think; just answer with the first thing that comes into your mind. Once you've got it, then ask yourself, "Now, how can I get there? How can I do the things I want to do in life?"

For me, mobile home investing has given me the time to do the things I want to do. Nowadays, I have time for traveling to new places, watching a good movie or going on a hiking trip without the management hassles I once had as a landlord. No longer do I receive calls for toilets that need to be fixed or air-conditioning units needing repair. Working with folks with a homeowner mentality is far more of a pleasant experience for me than working with those with a renter type of mentality. It is truly a passive investing system (passive in the sense that the payments keep coming in after the work is done). I have the best of both worlds: the payments come in just as in a landlording situation, yet I'm not responsible for home maintenance like I was as a landlord.

Step 2: Get Your Personal Finances in Order

There have been countless people who have invested in other people's homes without even having their own finances in order, and it's always a recipe for disaster. By having your financial house in order, you will know how much money is going in and how much money is going out. You'll know what areas you need to work on in your finances. These are basic concepts, yet many people are not fully aware of their own financial situation. It's very important to stay on top of your finances so that you will be able to see how you're progressing toward your overall goals.

(Note: At the end of this book, there is a "Resources" section listing books I recommend on personal finance.)

Short-Term Goals versus Long-Term Goals

Once you have your finances in order, you will need to figure out your goals. If you're planning to buy and hold, do you have the money and cash reserves needed for purchasing and acquiring properties? If not, how will you get there? Do you need to build up cash? If so, how much cash, and what is your time frame?

I recommend making both short-term and long-term

goals. For example, a short-term goal could be to learn your market and do your first mobile home deal within a certain period of time, say in the next six months. A long-term goal might be to create enough passive income within three years to cover your rent or mortgage payment so that you can work toward having your largest expense paid off every month by a passive income stream.

Remember, everyone has different goals and is at different stages in life. Whatever you decide your goals should be, they are your goals and your goals only. Do not be concerned with what anyone else is doing. Focus on what you want to do and the type of lifestyle you want to create for yourself, not what others want for you or for themselves.

Step 3: Do You Have the Money to Start Buying and Holding?

If you have little to no funds and cash reserves to start buying properties, I do not recommend starting to buy and hold properties. Despite what you may have read in courses out there, there will always be holding costs when buying and acquiring properties.

In this day and age, especially in this economy, you never know what will happen. It may take awhile to fill your properties, especially in the beginning with no experience. Success does not happen overnight, which is why it's very important to account for the issues that may come up in the future.

Believe me, these miscellaneous issues do come up. I'm talking from a property management point of view. You need to be prepared for the worst. The worst thing that could happen is putting in a bad buyer/tenant—one who does not pay. And even worse, a nonpaying buyer/tenant who does not take care of the home.

Remember, even though you sell the home to a buyer using owner financing/lease optioning, they still owe YOU money. If the payments are not coming in on a regular basis and if they do not take care of the home, you are going to be left with an asset in really bad shape. In finance, we call these "junk" assets.

As Murphy's Law says, "What can go wrong, will go wrong." Be prepared for the worst.

How Much Money Do I Need to Start?

Honestly, I cannot answer this question—it is different for everyone. You need to figure out first if you have the cash reserves to start acquiring properties in this business. The amount you will need will depend on your comfort level. Remember, you need to account not only for the purchase of the homes, but also the holding costs involved (e.g., fix-up work, lot rent, utilities, etc.).

If you do not have the funds to start, I recommend

going out and finding deals for other investors. Even if you do have the funds to start, it's really important to learn from those in your area who are already doing what you want to do. Every area is going to have a different way of doing things. By finding like-minded folks in your area, you create shortcuts and get to know more quickly how things are done, rather than trying to find everything out yourself. Remember, two heads are better than one.

(Note: I talk more about this in Chapter 11: Build Your Team.)

Building up Cash

Once you have figured out your finances, you need to set aside a certain amount on a regular basis for investing. Many personal finance books recommend a minimum of 10 percent of your gross income. If you have money left over, you may want to set aside more.

(Note: Remember that the "Recommended Resources" section at the end of this book lists recommended books on personal finance.)

Even if your plan is first to build up cash by finding deals for other investors, you're going to need some start-up money. Every business needs funds to start up, and the real estate business is no exception. You will need to set aside some funds for basic office start-up expenses (discussed in the next chapter), as well as marketing expenses. If you need to, create a budget. And stick to it!

Next, figure out whether you plan to look for deals yourself or enlist the aid of others to find deals for you. If you decide to enlist others' help, then you will also need to figure in the numbers for partnering and/or compensating others for their services.

(Note: Be sure to check the local laws in your area regarding compensation for referrals. Each locale has different laws on this issue.)

Chapter 6

Setting up Your Office

There are a few essential items for starting up a mobile home investment office, but significantly fewer than with most businesses. In the beginning, I highly recommend that you keep things as simple as possible. Only spend money on items you need, not the extras that you just want.

In my experience, it does not take a lot of money to set up a basic office. If you are just starting out, here are my recommendations on the basic essential items and equipment you are going to need:

1. Basic Computer

Depending on how you work, this can be a desktop computer or a laptop. Personally, I do not carry around a laptop with me. In the beginning, I thought I would need to carry a laptop everywhere I went. I pictured myself drawing up contracts from a laptop while meeting with a seller or a buyer/tenant, and even looked into purchasing a portable printer. In practice, though, I have found that the degree of mobility a laptop provides is really not necessary. Again, I think this is a personal choice.

2.   Cell Phone

Cell phone service is a must in this business. A basic phone is fine—it doesn't have to be a smartphone. In the past, I've also had a dedicated office line, but it did not work out for me and was very costly. It was too hard to keep track of two phones with two different voice mail messages. Sometimes people were not able to reach me at one number because I was either not at that phone or did not receive the message in a timely fashion. Having two different numbers is just plain unnecessary and confusing. Sellers and buyers should be able to get hold of you wherever you are, and it's easier for everyone if they only have to keep track of a single number. If you are on a really tight budget, I recommend using your cell phone for all your calls. You can set up a Google Voice number to forward all calls to your cell phone so you can have one dedicated work number for your business.

3.   Office Supplies

Be sure to have basic office supplies before you start. At a minimum, have a notebook (to take notes, log seller/buyer calls, etc.), pens, paper, paper clips, etc. Before you start out, make sure you have the basic necessities of running your office. *(Note: For those interested, I have created a sample checklist for essential items in "Setting up Your Office" in Appendix 1.)*

4.   Financial Calculator

Having a good financial calculator comes very handy in this business. So do you need a real calculator? Or does a software program work? Again, it's all a matter of personal preference, but I find that having a physical calculator is a great backup tool even if you normally rely on a software program for your calculations. Personally, I have a $29.99 Hewlett Packard 10B II personal financial calculator that I carry around with me. Take the time to learn how to fully use your calculator before you need it.

5.   Marketing Materials

When first starting out, it's best to have some basic marketing materials, such as business cards, flyers, etc., that you will use to market yourself. Don't forget to buy some tacks and a good staple gun as well to post up your marketing materials on bulletin boards in your area.

6.   Digital Camera

Having a digital camera is a must in this business. In the beginning, I relied on my notes and my memory to remember the homes that I had inspected. However, after inspecting many mobile homes, I soon could not remember which homes were which just based on my notes. Sometimes I forgot what the homes had looked like, or I forgot the types of repairs that needed to be done. By having a digital camera and taking pictures of homes when I inspect them, it's easier for me to remember the homes since I have the pictures with me. The saying "Pictures are worth a thousand words" really rings true when it comes to inspecting mobile homes.

7.   Other Items

These are the bare essentials that you'll need to start up your office. Depending on your personal preferences and needs, you may choose to buy other items as well. A sample checklist of items you may find useful to your office is included in Appendix 1.

Set up Your Office to Cater to Your Personality

Personally, I keep my office really simple. I'm not much of a technology person—I'm more of a paper and pen kind of gal. So I keep things simple and don't bother using the latest and greatest technology tools to run my office.

In the past, I have tried to implement new technology in my business, thinking the effort it took to learn it would pay off in the end. But I found that I just never became comfortable with it, and as a result did not use it. It's just not my style. If you like new technology and are good at picking it up, the technology is out there, but if it's not your style I am living proof that it's not necessary for success in the mobile home investing business. Again, it's all a matter of personality. Set up your office according to your personality and how you prefer to do things, not how others do.

Chapter 7

Business Basics

Do I Need to Form a Business Entity?

If you are new to the business, I always recommend folks try it out first before making the decision to formally form an entity. It is not necessary to form a business entity before doing your first deal, so what's the rush? I mean, really, what if you do your first mobile home deal only to find out from the experience that this business is not for you? Then what?

If you've formed an entity for the business already when you discover it's not for you, you've wasted a lot of money, not to mention time spent thinking up a name and working on the logistics. Some people assume they're going to like the business, but there's no harm in taking it slow. Honestly, you may like or not like this business. Personally, I know countless people who have tried out the business of buying, selling and financing/lease optioning used mobile homes, only to find out it was not for them.

There are so many factors that make this business appealing, but so many factors that make it unappealing too.

So try it out first. Do a deal or two. See if you enjoy this business and decide if it's right for you. If you do not feel comfortable conducting a business on your own and feel you must form a business entity before starting out, then by all means do what makes you feel comfortable. Eventually, if you do decide to form a business entity after finding out this business is for you, some of the pluses include tax benefits, such as the ability to deduct certain expenses and write things off, in addition to possible liability protection, depending on what structure you choose. I am not giving you legal or financial advice; this is just my personal opinion based on my experience.

Dealer's License

Some areas require you to obtain a dealer's license if you are going to buy and sell mobile homes. Check with your local housing authority on this issue. Of course, you are going to have to work within the laws of your area. In some areas, you're not required to get a license until you have done a certain number of transactions.

(Note: The dealer's license issue usually pertains to those who are buying and selling mobile homes. If you are planning to buy and hold homes to rent, this issue usually does not apply.)

Should I Get a Dealer's License When First Starting Out?

Of course, if your area requires you to obtain a dealer's license to buy and sell even one mobile home, then you should. If not, I again recommend trying things out before making a commitment for the long term.

Chapter 8

Educate Yourself

There are numerous books and materials out there on mobile home investing. And it's very important to educate yourself not only on the mechanics of mobile home investing, but also on the sales and psychology of being a mobile home investor.

As I've mentioned before, I highly recommend *Deals on Wheels* by Lonnie Scruggs (often referred to as "The Godfather" of mobile home investing). In his book, Lonnie explains step by step how he came to discover this little niche of investing, as well as why he enjoys it so much. I believe Lonnie laid out the blueprint for what we see today in mobile home investing when it comes to buying, selling and financing used mobile homes.

Apart from Lonnie Scruggs' materials, there are a number of other books out there on mobile home investing, all of which have something to offer. By reading them, you'll get other perspectives on the business. I have made a list of other recommended mobile home investing materials in the back of this book.

Psychology and Marketing

Apart from reading about the logistics of mobile home investing, I feel it is very important to learn about the psychology and skills involved in mobile home investing and selling. Let's face it, running a business involves people skills. There are different types of people out there.

For me, my success has been a direct result of how I approach people, listen to their problems and offer solutions to help them. Above all else, it's all in the presentation. It's not what you say, but how you say it that counts. And how you say things can be the difference between putting a deal together or not. It's that important.

So make it a point to educate yourself on the psychology of sales and marketing. There are numerous books out there on the subject. One book I highly recommend is *Influence* by Robert Cialdini. It's a very interesting and informative read on how and why people make their buying decisions. I've read it numerous times, and get something new and valuable from it each time.

(Note: For those interested, I've made a list of recommended books in the "Resources" section at the back of this book.)

Audio Books while Driving in the Car

In addition to reading about mobile home investing, I feel audio books are a great way to do two things at the same time: drive to where you need to be and get educated. Let me tell you, there is a lot of driving done in this business.

Personally, I try to listen to one or two audio books per month. If money is tight, check out your local library to see what types of audio books they have available. You might be surprised by their selection—I know I have been.

You might also consider signing up for a subscription service such as Audible.com if you plan to be an active listener of audio books. Or you can always just purchase the ones you're interested in.

Always Keep Learning

My point is that you should always be educating yourself. After you read or listen to one book, I highly recommend just taking some time to think about it. And if you feel it's necessary, read and/or listen to it again. It's always interesting to me to discover the new things I learn on a second, third or fourth read. I guess it's true what they say: we do learn by repetition.

Chapter 9

Learn Your Market

Before you start making offers on mobile homes, it's important to learn your market. You need to find out what homes are worth on their own (i.e., wholesale value, retail value [including cash value and owner finance value, etc.]), what homes are worth in parks (this usually varies on a park-by-park basis), etc.

How Can I Learn the Market?

So how do you learn your market? Go out and see lots of mobile homes. When I first started out, I visited parks, mobile home dealerships, homes on land and homes on lots. Before I even did my first deal, I must have gone and inspected hundreds of mobile homes.

Yes, this did take a lot of time, not to mention a lot of driving (and, as you know from the prior chapter, a lot of learning through audio books). But in the end I came out with the knowledge and experience I needed to know my market. And that is priceless.

Inspecting all those homes taught me the values of

homes depending on the size, age, amount of work done, location, etc. And I was able to take this knowledge and apply it to real life.

I recommend that you do the same—visit a lot of mobile home parks, mobile home dealerships, mobile homes on land and mobile homes on lots. Look at nice homes in nice areas, nice homes in not-so-nice areas, bad homes in nice areas and bad homes in not-so-nice areas. Compare them and their values.

What Are the Different Sizes and Dimensions of Mobile Homes?

Most mobile homes will come in the following configurations: two bedrooms/one bath, two bedrooms/two bath, three bedrooms/one bath and three bedrooms/two baths. Four bedrooms/two baths exist, but they are rare. When you get into double wides, you'll even encounter an occasional five-bedroom.

Regarding the sizes of the homes, the older homes (from the 1980s and earlier) are usually going to be either 12 feet or 14 feet wide by 50, 60 or 70 feet long. The much older ones can be smaller; I've seen a 10 x 50 before, but I hesitate to recommend buying these homes, as they are really old and small. Unless there is a demand for this type and size of home in your area, I would stay away.

Personally, I prefer newer homes from the 1990s and

2000s. Usually, these homes are 16 feet in width by 56, 66 or 76 feet in length (add 4 feet for the hitch).

Most of these homes will either have aluminum siding or wood siding. My preference is aluminum, though I've been able to work with homes with wood siding. The issue with wood siding is the boards need to be replaced on a regular basis, depending on the weather conditions of the area. Wood will start to rot when exposed to moisture, while aluminum will not.

Single Wides versus Double Wides

In the beginning, I recommend sticking with single wide mobile homes. Single wide mobile homes have only one (single) section, whereas double wides have two sections (double in width).

Personally, I've found that single wide mobile homes are much easier to work with, and are usually less costly than double wides. Again, this is going to depend on your market.

In my experience, most folks who are looking do not mind a single wide as long as the demand meets it in your area. If you are planning to sell mobile homes using owner financing, it has been my experience that most folks will be able to pay the same amount as a down payment and the same amount as a monthly payment for either a single wide or a double wide. Again, be sure to check the market demand in your area.

Documenting Your Mobile Home Adventures

After seeing many homes, you will get a sense of the values of homes in the area. I highly recommend keeping a notebook with the addresses (including part of town) and specs of each home you visit. You'll also want to ask a lot of questions when you're visiting a mobile home. Ask the dealer or the homeowner what homes have sold in that area. If you are working in a park, ask the park manager what homes have sold in that particular park and how long ago (i.e., is there a current demand?).

Write these figures down. Write everything down. Be sure to date your entry. Do not rely on your memory, as sometimes we forget details over time. I know I have.

There have been times when I've written things down, only to refer back to my notes after several months or years and surprise myself when I read what I wrote. Sometimes I forget certain situations and how they turned out. By rereading what I write, I'm able to revisit the past. For example, there was a time when I reread an entry I made about a home I went to see in a particular park. Now, this home needed a lot of work. So I made a list of what needed to be done and consulted with the park manager. At the time, the park manager had given me a list of costs associated with fix-up work involved with mobile homes based on his experience when fixing up his own homes. This list had helped me to determine how much it would cost for the work involved when asking for bids from contractors. I had completely forgotten about this list, only to realize I was overpaying for some of the work I had done! This is the power of writing things down. We learn by repetition. If you keep writing the same details down over and over again, such as size and type of mobile homes you see in a particular area, you will start to notice patterns. And these patterns will help you to learn the market.

Knowledge is power. By learning the market, you will gain the knowledge that will set you light speed ahead of the rest of the pack when opportunities arise.

(Note: In the back of this book, I have an example worksheet of what types of information you need to find out about mobile homes when learning your market.)

Chapter 10

Have an Exit Strategy

Before you even start to invest and find leads, you need to have an exit strategy. Having an exit strategy beforehand will guide you when you are faced with opportunities. With each lead you find, you really need to know what you are going to do before going in. Will you buy and sell retail? Will you buy and sell wholesale? Will you buy and sell "as-is"? Or will you buy and sell to fix up? Will you buy and rent? Or will you sell to another investor to build up cash? So many times, I've seen investors just kind of "wing it" with a "we'll see what happens" mentality.

Well, I'm here to tell you that a "we'll see what happens" mentality can get you into a whole lot of trouble. Believe me, I know. You need to have an exit strategy for everything that you do, and that includes mobile home investing.

For example, I know of one investor who purchased a mobile home and did not have an exit strategy. This investor tried to "wing it" and was not sure what she would do if the mobile home purchase came through.

At first, she wanted to sell the property retail for cash "as-is." But after awhile with no takers, she decided to try to wholesale the home. Then she changed her mind, and tried to sell owner finance. Then she tried to rent it out.

By the time this investor finally did anything with the home, it had been eight months. Can you believe that? Eight months of a property being vacant and not doing anything. All because she did not have an exit strategy. In the end, she ended up renting the home in an effort to fill it, as money was running low. She soon became a burnt-out landlord. Going in, she should have decided what she wanted to do based on her goals and stuck with it. This is why it's so important to really know your goals and have an exit strategy.

Write Down Your Exit Strategy before You Start

I highly recommend you write down your exit strategy before you start investing and looking for leads. Have a time frame in mind. For example, if your goal is to build up cash before you can start buying and holding, give yourself a figure to work with.

Let's say you decide to build up $10,000. In this case, when you buy a mobile home, you'll want to sell it quickly for cash rather than to buy and hold. Your exit strategy would involve building up cash with each lead you find until you reach your goal of $10,000. You also need to give yourself a time frame to reach your goals.

Let's say one year. (Note: Remember, you want to be as realistic as possible.)

And let's say you want to get paid at least $1,000 for each mobile home you sell and/or locate for other investors. That would mean to get to your goal, you would need to locate at least ten mobile homes. Can you do it? It's up to you.

What if I Find a Good Deal to Buy and Hold?

Some people say, "Well, if I find a good deal that I want to keep, I'm going to keep it." I know this because I've said the same thing myself. It's very tempting to want to keep some deals that come your way, especially if you're constantly finding them for other investors.

However, I know now that it's not a good idea. When you buy and hold, issues start to come up that cost both time and money. This may include plumbing issues, such as a toilet not working properly or a sink leaking, electrical and mechanical issues, such as air-conditioning units stopping, or even simple landscaping issues, such as the grass and trees needing to be trimmed and cut. When you're tempted to hold, it's really important to keep your goals in mind. Once you start deviating from your goals, you start to lose focus. It's happened to me.

If you are going to buy and hold properties (this includes selling on owner finance/lease option), you really need to have a good cash reserve as well as a good team. Why? So that when the issues start to come up that inevitably will come up, you'll know who to call.

If your exit strategy is just to get paid to find and locate deals for other investors, then you are in and out of deals fairly quickly. However, if your exit strategy is to buy and hold—either by renting out or selling on owner finance/lease option—you are in it for the long haul. If this is the case, you need to have all your ducks lined up. Otherwise, it's going to end up costing a lot of time and a lot of money.

Having an exit strategy is very important. In the back of the book, I have an exit strategy and goal worksheet that you may use to plan for these aspects of your business. In addition to having an exit strategy, you will also need to have a good team.

Chapter 11

Build Your Team

Having a good team is an essential part of being successful in this business. We've all heard the saying "Two heads are better than one." Well, it's true, and more than two is better yet. Having others you can call upon to advise you, help you out of a tough spot or provide services you'll need is invaluable.

How to Build Your Team

So how do you go about building your team? Well, it starts with a plan. The type of team you build will depend on your goals. Look back at your short-term and long-term goals. Figure out what you'll need from others in order to accomplish these goals, and from there figure out what sort of team members you need to locate.

For example, if you are looking for mobile home deals for other investors, your list may be different from if you are starting to buy and acquire properties. The former would focus solely on team members and strategies to help find leads, such as park managers and mobile home dealerships, while the latter would also include team members for support out of necessity, including contractors to help with fix-up work and insurance agents to provide insurance on homes. If you are looking to purchase mobile homes in parks, your team members may be different (or the same) from if you are looking to purchase mobile homes on land and/or lots. Finding mobile homes in parks requires relationships with park managers, while finding homes on land and/or lots involves building relationships with real estate agents and/or mobile home dealerships in the area.

If you are just starting out, here is my recommended list of essential team members to have on your team:

1.   Personal support network (friends, spouse, other investors, etc.)

It's very important to have a personal support network of people who understand you and your investing goals. Surround yourself with like-minded people. Get away from the naysayers. Now, I know this is easier said than done, because many people (especially family and sometimes friends) may not understand why you have entered this crazy world of mobile home investing. Seek out people who do understand (e.g., a local real estate club, other local clubs, real estate blogs, Internet sites, etc.). If you surround yourself with like-minded people, it will be easier for you to go out and take action, and they will be able to support you emotionally when you need it.

2.   Mentor

Whenever I want to learn something new, I have always sought out a mentor. It's very important to have someone locally you can learn from. I stress locally because laws, marketing, rents, etc. are different in every area. What works in one area may not work in another. Seek out someone who is doing what you want to do; learn from that person and offer to help him or her find deals in return. Create a win/win situation. Make it work for both of you. Believe me, the information you learn will be invaluable and will give you leverage, which equals speed in this business.

3.   Park Managers

If you are planning to work with parks, you will need to establish relationships with park managers. They are a great source of information. Apart from educating you about the park and how they operate, park managers can help you to learn more about the mobile home business and the market in your area. If you are planning to do business in mobile home parks, park managers are definitely important members to have on your team.

4.   Mobile Home Dealerships

Mobile home dealerships are also key players to have on your mobile home investing team. They can educate you on the market and tell you exactly how much they have sold their homes in the area for. Sometimes they may even get homes that come in for "trade-ins" and may need someone to off-load the homes for them.

For the most part, mobile home dealerships are in the business of selling new homes, not used homes. It's just like a car dealership—their clients buy new, sometimes trading in the old for the new. If you are there to help off-load the old, you are helping them to focus on their business of selling new homes.

5.   Contractors

You'll always need contractors on your mobile home investing team. For the major systems in the home (e.g., electrical, plumbing, air-conditioning, etc.), be sure to work with a licensed contractor. Also, you will need a handyman on your team to fix up the small items and for minor repairs. Be sure to have a few contractors in each area of expertise, just in case you need backups in a pinch. Remember, you do not want to be looking for contractors when you need the job done. Start networking now!

6.   Cleaning Crew

In most cases, the mobile homes you buy will need a good cleaning. Be sure to have a cleaning crew lined up, as well as some backups for tougher cleaning jobs. Though it can get pricey at times, it really is worth hiring a crew for a job well done. These folks know what they are doing and have educated me quite a bit about the professional cleaning product world. They have also recommended some great products. The education alone is priceless!

7.   Carpet Cleaners

Another major area of mobile homes that may need cleaning is the carpet. Sure, you can have your cleaning crew clean the carpets if they don't look that bad, but if it looks like a tough job, I usually go with professional carpet cleaners who specialize in this area. It's amazing to see what carpet cleaners can do. At times, their work has made carpets look like new!

8.   Mobile Home Movers

If you are planning to buy mobile homes and move them, you will need a mobile home mover on your team. Usually, I check around with the mobile home dealerships and mobile home park managers to see whom they use. Talk to and interview a few mobile home movers, get their rates and make sure they are licensed. You can verify licensing information through your local government authority.

9.   Local Government Authority

Speaking of which, getting acquainted with the people who work at your local government authority in charge of handling mobile home transactions can help you with your mobile home investing business. These people are familiar with the ins and outs of the logistics and paperwork involved in the mobile home business in your area. They can help guide you, but remember they cannot give legal advice. They are also a wealth of information for local mobile home–related resources, including finding out the licensing status of mobile home movers, contractors, etc.

10. Other Real Estate Investors

Having other real estate investors on your team can be very important to your mobile home investing career. Real estate investors can be great sources of information for other services you may need, including attorneys, real estate agents, contractors, etc. They may also have access to buyer and seller leads. There are many ways you can meet other investors, including attending your local real estate club, calling other investors who advertise in the paper, visiting location sites, etc.

Always be open to creating relationships with other investors.

11. Insurance Agent

One of the most valuable members of my team is my insurance agent. If you are planning to buy and hold, it is extremely important to have a good insurance agent on your team who is knowledgeable in the mobile home business. My insurance agent specializes in mobile homes and does not do anything else. It is extremely important to work with an insurance agent who understands your business. Even when a home is vacant, I put insurance on it just in case. I recommend you do the same. As the saying goes, "It's better to be safe than sorry."

Start Networking Early and Choose Your Team Wisely

Remember, networking takes time, so start now. Figure out your exit strategy and start finding team members to help you. Do not wait until you need these services; that is the worst position to be in!

I mentioned earlier that I've learned always to have backup team members for each service category. For example, if I need a handyman I will interview a few and choose at least three to have on hand. I'll decide on my top choice, middle and bottom—just in case one is not available. It's always good to have a backup because you never know what will happen.

Do not rely on one person to do the job, even if that person is dependable most of the time. As I have learned, there could be a time when that person may not be available and/or there may be someone else who is just as good or even better who may offer competitive rates. Remember, the person who has the most interest in your business is YOU. If you take care of your business, your business will take care of you.

In any case, this is a minimal list of team members to help you get started in the mobile home business. Again, your personal list of team members will depend on your goals.

(Note: At the back of this book, I have a checklist of team members you may need, depending on what your exit strategy is.)

Chapter 12

Finding Mobile Home Parks to Work With

If you are new to the mobile home business, the best way to start out, in my opinion, is to work in mobile home parks. Why? The reason I recommend working in parks versus buying homes out on land and/or lots is because mobile home parks already have a community of people living there. If there are people already living in a park, you know there is a market and a need for housing in that area.

On the other hand, the supply and demand of homes on land and/or lots may not be so obvious. These homes may be more spread out and may not have a sense of community that mobile home parks have to offer. In these situations, determining the demand is difficult if the homes are more scarce and farther apart. Your market will be limited. One of the worst things that can happen is finding a home and not having a buyer. And the ultimate worst thing that can happen is having a home and putting in the wrong type of buyer. Having the wrong type of people in a home can be disastrous should they fall behind on payments or damage the home. This is why it's very important to find parks to work with that you feel comfortable working in.

Just like single family homes and residential real estate, where there are different types of neighborhoods, there are also different types of mobile home parks. Certain parks attract a certain clientele. The type of clientele a park attracts will highly depend on the park's presentation. The best way to find out what kind of clientele parks attract is to go out and visit the parks.

Finding Mobile Home Parks in Your Area

So how do you find parks in your area? The best way is to do an Internet search. I recommend Google Maps (maps.google.com). Type "mobile home parks" in the search field, and a list of parks in your area will come up. Print out this list and keep it with you.

Now, I have to warn you that not all parks will show up on the map. I've found many parks by accident, just by driving through the areas where I choose to work. Sometimes I've found other parks by talking to residents of the parks in which I'm working.

Once you have a list of the parks in your area, I highly recommend you drive to ALL of them. This will allow you to compare them firsthand. You will see low-end parks, you will see middle-of-the-road parks and you will see high-end parks.

Personally, I work high-end parks because I feel comfortable with the types of clientele they attract. People who are buying or selling a house in a high-end park are more likely to make payments on time, to keep the home in nice condition, etc.

So how do you determine what's a low-end park, middle-of-the-road park and high-end park? A lot of it is gut instinct. When you drive into a park, you will get a feeling about the park and the types of people who live there. Look around. How does the park make you feel? Do you feel safe? Or does it feel dangerous? Just by driving through the park, you will see how the community is operated and what is allowed and not allowed.

High-End Parks

In most high-end parks, you will not see any fences and large dogs outside. Most of these parks only allow small inside dogs. In addition, high-end parks usually have amenities such as a clubhouse, swimming pool, basketball courts, etc. One of the high-end parks I work with even has a dog park—amazing! You'll also know it's a high-end park because of the way the residents and the park management take care of the park and the homes—they care. Pride of ownership will show.

Low-End Parks

Low-end parks will not have many of the amenities you'll see in high-end parks (e.g., dog park, pool, basketball court, etc.), though I have visited low-end parks with some amenities. In a low-end park, you will mostly see beat-up cars, homes that are not taken care of, large dogs behind fences, and even some dogs and/or cats walking around loose. I have been chased before by large dogs in low-end parks. Watch out and be careful when walking through these parks.

Middle-of-the-Road Parks

Middle-of-the-road parks will be just that—right in between. They will not be as nice as high-end parks, but not as unkempt as low-end parks. Sometimes middle-of-the-road parks do not have paved roads. I've found that many of these parks are out in rural areas. For me, they are OK to work in as long as I still feel comfortable with the type of clientele they attract, though they are not the parks I prefer.

Why I Prefer High-End Parks

High-end parks have very strict criteria on whom they allow in their parks, as well as strict rules for residents to maintain the outside appearance of their homes. Some may consider these rules a negative, as it limits the market for clientele. Personally, I think it's a positive—it shows the park cares about the community. They don't allow just anyone into their park. And that is very important, especially for the residents.

In fact, I'd go so far as to say that working in high-end parks has been the key to my success. When I first started out, I really did not see the differences between the different types of parks. Back then, all I saw were the homes, and all that mattered was putting deals together. I learned the hard way the importance of picking and choosing which parks to work with and which parks not to work with.

My $2,000 Nightmare

To illustrate why I no longer pursue low-end parks, I'll share with you a story about something that happened to me when I was getting started in mobile home investing. The park manager in a low-end park was really pushing me to buy homes in his park. And it was really tempting, because there were a lot of cheap homes. Thing is, I was warned by the other park managers in the area that this park had a bad reputation—the park didn't care about their residents. And it showed—there were potholes in the street, loose dogs, unkempt yards, broken-down fences and deteriorating board paneling on homes. The list goes on and on. It just was not my type of park. But I went ahead with the deal anyway.

In this situation, I went against my gut feeling (never do this!) and based my decision to buy in the park solely on price. In the end, I paid dearly for it.

I had a stack of applications from folks who were interested, but none of them met my criteria. I typically look for people who have a stable work and landlord history. Those who change jobs or move residences in a short period of time are a red flag for transient types. I am looking for those who can demonstrate stability for the long term. I knew the folks who were applying were not the type of clientele I wanted to work with—I just did not feel comfortable. I made the decision that I had to get out of this situation and get out of this park. So I took a loss—I left the mobile home and with it, the $2,000 I had paid for it. It was a large price to pay, but I learned my lesson—I will never deal in low-end parks again.

What Types of Parks Should You Work With?

Am I saying you shouldn't deal in low-end parks? No. I'm saying you need to work in parks in which you feel comfortable working. I know many investors whose bread and butter business exists in low-end parks—and they are very successful. Some people are comfortable working in these types of parks and with the types of clientele they attract. But if you are not, then don't.

After you have driven around to many parks, you'll

want to choose the ones you feel comfortable working with. Again, this is a personal choice, so do what makes you feel comfortable.

Chapter 13

Working with the Park Manager

Once you have chosen the parks you'd like to work in, you'll need to go in and build rapport with the park manager. This is very important. Do not start pursuing homes in a park without first building a relationship with the park manager. Why? If you do find a home you want to buy and keep in the park, it will be much easier to do if you know the park manager beforehand. The general public does not like the word "investor." In my opinion, investors have a bad name and bad connotation. If the park manager knows you first and you have a good relationship, you'll be a lot more likely to be allowed to invest in his or her park. Relationships are the key to success in this business.

How to Talk to the Park Manager

So when you go in to see the manager, what do you say? Say you are there only for information. Remember that. Do not go in saying you are an investor and you do this and you do that. Do not ask the park manager for referrals for homes to buy in the park. This is a big mistake.

I see so many investors taking an "I'm the high almighty" attitude—they talk above the managers, not to them on the same level. This is the quickest way to turn off a park manager, and he or she will not allow you to work in the park. When approaching park managers, the best thing to do is to be pleasant. Usually, they will greet you and ask, "How may I help you?"

What I Say When I Visit Park Managers for the First Time

When I first visit park managers, I usually smile, say hi and tell them I was driving by and noticed the park. At this point, they may start telling you more about the park and its amenities. Let them talk. Do not try to dominate the conversation. You need to learn to be a good listener.

If the park manager does not say anything, I usually just tell him or her I just came by to get more information about the park. And that's it.

From there, again, let the manager do all the talking. Remember, you are there for information. If you keep that in mind, you will do fine. Do not think you will get any leads and/or referrals from a park manager on your first visit—it's just not going to happen. Relationships take time to build, but once a strong relationship has been built, it will pay off in the end.

Write Everything Down

When visiting park managers, be sure to go in with a pen and a notebook. Jot down all the information the park manager tells you, including lot rent amount, amenities, electricity, water, etc.

Go in with the mentality of a homeowner. Ask questions that a homeowner would ask. Learn to just "go with the flow" in your conversation. Give yourself a good two hours with the park manager—do not rush it.

Once the park manager has told you all the information about the park, then and only then do you want to go into what you do and why you are there. Again, I do not recommend you use the word "investor" when you talk to the park manager—it just has a bad connotation and leaves a bad taste in many people's mouths.

Remember, building rapport is more of an art than a science. It's not what you say but how you say it that counts. So when you're ready to go into why you're there and what you do, be careful about how you present yourself.

Usually, I will just say that I help people get financing on used mobile homes. Don't go into too much detail; just keep things simple. Surely, you do not want to confuse the park manager with words he or she is unfamiliar with and logistical details. Prepare what you are going to say to the simplest level, because some park managers will have much more of an understanding of what you do than others. Remember, you just want to make them feel comfortable with you.

At this point, the park manager will probably be surprised and interested (if you did a good job of building rapport). I've had many park managers say, "Well, that's great. We have many people who try to sell their homes here who can't find a lender for their buyers. You will be a great fit and asset to the park." This will be the beginning of a new relationship.

Again, it's not what you say, but how you say it that counts. You need to practice, practice, practice how you talk to people, because if you are there superficially and don't have the right intent, others can see and feel it. You need to be sincere in your approach. If you're not, your experience is going to be very frustrating.

What if the Park Manager Won't Let You Work in the Park?

Will there be park managers who say you cannot work there even after you talk to them? Yes. But most won't.

As I discussed at the beginning of this book, when I first started out, a park manager told me I could not work in her park. Out of the hundreds of parks I've visited, that remains the only park that has told me no, and the reason was that they only rented homes. So that was that.

Don't take it personally if you get a no. If a park manager tells you you can't work in his or her park, just thank the manager for his or her time and move on. Sooner or later, you will find a park that is open to doing business with you. It just takes persistence and time.

In the back of this book, I've included a sample work-sheet outlining my approach when first meeting park managers.

Chapter 14

Marketing: Finding Sellers

Once you've decided which parks you'd like to work in and built a relationship with the park managers, the next step is to start meeting sellers. The most important thing in this business is to be in front of people. When first talking to sellers, it does not matter what the price is or the condition of the home—what matters is that you go out there and get the experience of being in front of the sellers. This is a people business.

The reason I mention this is because there are so many investors out there who try to buy homes without ever meeting the sellers—they try to negotiate purely over the phone.

From my experience, it's nearly impossible (unless the seller is desperate) to negotiate a price and buy a home over the phone. Plus, you need to be asking yourself not "How can I get this home?" but, "Is this the kind of home I want to buy?" When you approach a sale from that perspective, it becomes a whole different ballgame—and that's not an approach it's possible to take over the phone.

Marketing to Sellers

You may be wondering how to market to sellers. In the beginning, you're going to have to do a lot of trial and error. Without a doubt, the best sources of leads are park managers, but these leads only come over time as you build a relationship with the park managers. It's usually only after you've done a couple deals in a particular park that the manager will start referring leads to you on a regular basis. In the beginning, it is up to you to go out and find opportunities. Let people you talk to know what you do—once enough people know what you do, then the opportunities will start to find you.

Aside from relationship building, there are a couple of good marketing strategies that may help you, which I'll explain below. I highly suggest you tailor your marketing strategy to your personality and skill set. Don't force yourself to do things that you do not like to do. Only do things that you feel comfortable doing. By focusing on your strengths and not your weaknesses, you'll use your time more effectively. Build your business around yourself; don't try to build yourself around your business.

Driving Parks

In the beginning, driving around in mobile home parks is a really good way to get to know the park and find sellers in the park. Many sellers will put a For Sale By Owner sign in front of their home—it's just common sense. I recommend driving the parks you want to work in and finding every FSBO sign you can. Call them up and visit every single one of them.

Now, I know some out there may say, "But why ALL of them? Why not only the ones that are priced right?" The reason I say this is because the asking price over the phone does not matter. Deals are made through building relationships, and often the price of a home may end up being a lot lower than the asking price. You cannot adequately build a relationship through just one phone call.

So when you call sellers, get only the basic information about the house during the phone call (there is a script in the back of this book), and then visit every single one of them. Believe me, it will be a good experience for you. You will learn a lot about the market, the park and about inspecting mobile homes.

Most investors will not take the time to visit homes that do not fall in their price range. To me, this is a big mistake. Most of the homes that I've bought have started out with asking prices at or above retail value, but I went to see these homes anyway. It was not until I developed a relationship with these sellers that I was able to create a deal that was a win/win situation for everyone.

Do not make the same mistake as other investors. If

you take the time to go out and meet sellers despite the asking price of the home, you will learn a lot and have an edge over those who do not. The experience will give you knowledge, and as I keep emphasizing, knowledge is power.

Park Managers

As I mentioned earlier, the best source of leads is working with park managers. In the beginning, visit the park managers whenever you are in the park just to say hi. Even if it's a very quick visit, the more the park managers and their staff see and get to know you, the more you will be engrained in their minds. When you go to visit them, don't just focus on "Do you have any leads?" Really get to know the park, the staff and their likes/dislikes. People enjoy working with those who care. Take the extra time to care for others, and they will care for you.

Flyers

Passing out flyers and posting them in areas where you want to work is also a good way to get the word out. In the beginning, I passed out flyers in the streets to people walking around the parks I was interested in. You can learn a lot just by conversing with others, both about what is going on in the park and about the types of people who live there. And the people who live in parks most likely have friends and relatives who also live in parks, and who may be looking to buy or sell.

You might also consider posting flyers on bulletin boards in local businesses near the parks. Try to find a few Laundromats (which are great places to post flyers because people have time to read them while waiting for their clothes) and local restaurants, libraries, schools, gas stations, etc.

Now, how do you find these bulletin boards? I used to call around, but many employees were apathetic and said they didn't know. Usually, they would tell me to call back or put me on hold, never to get back to me. The best method is just to drive around the parks until you find the bulletin boards. In the beginning, I made a list of all the Laundromats and libraries in my area, then visited all of them and left my flyers there. In this business, I find it's best to go in person and get to know the businesses in the area just as a local would.

Signs

Check your local city ordinance to see if there are rules regarding posting signs in your area. A lot of times, people put up signs on busy street corners and large intersections for garage sales for the weekend, and then take them down before the start of the week. If this is allowed in your area, you can do the same. Usually, I will only place signs in areas where others' signs are. That's just me. My reasoning is if these signs are allowed to be here, then so can mine. If there are no signs there, I'm not sure it's allowed.

Personally, I use signs at a minimum, and only around parks I work in. I do not put much focus on this type of marketing; my main marketing focus is on networking since I am more of a people person. Again, do what you feel comfortable doing, and don't try to be something you're not.

Ads in Local Papers

Having an ad in a local paper or publication is another way to get the word out about what you do. This type of marketing does require money, but some investors find that it pays off. Smaller, free papers are good places to advertise. Again, you want to be where your clientele is—advertise in the types of papers that your clientele reads.

For an ad to be effective, it needs to run on a consistent basis. Some investors have told me they have tried to run ads in the local papers, but were unsuccessful at attracting new business. When I asked them how long they ran the ads for, I found it was only for a short period of time. If you are going to run an ad in the paper, you need to be in it for the long haul, giving potential buyers and sellers time to recognize your ad and think of you when they're looking to make a deal. I recommend running an ad for at least six months to measure results.

The good thing about running an ad in a paper is that it's there marketing you even when you're not out marketing yourself. However, the downside is that you don't know who is reading the ad.

I've received many calls from companies selling products and services from my ads. However, I've also gotten some really good leads that way. If you decide to go the ad route, I highly suggest you take the time to answer the phone when it rings or hire an answering service that can. The majority of people who call an ad only to find that no one answers will not leave voice mails, but will just go on to the next one.

Online Services Such as Craigslist

There are investors who swear by using Craigslist. In my experience, this has not been the best route to find sellers, though it's one worth trying (since it's free) if you're willing to take the time to weed through the leads. Whether you find it helpful or not in the end, it will give you experience, as you will encounter many different types of situations.

There are two ways to use Craigslist to help your business. You can put up a free posting that says you buy mobile homes for cash. If you plan to buy only in a particular area and/or park, I recommend you specify this in your ad. Also, if you do not want to buy homes on land and/or homes that need to be moved, I would also mention that in your ad. Unfortunately, these specifications may detract a lot of folks. If you make your ad as general as possible, you'll be more likely to get interest. The amount of interest you generate through your ad will get you going and give you the experience you need to build up your confidence and learn the market.

The other way you can use Craigslist for your business is to look for ads by sellers of mobile homes. When you see an ad that interests you, contact the person either by phone (which is faster) or email. Again, get the details and then decide whether to go out and see the home. If the home is in a park where you do not wish to work, I would only go to see the home if you plan on moving it. If not, skip it altogether rather than working in an area where you don't feel comfortable.

Craigslist may be effective if used properly. In my experience, though, I've found it to be filled with unmotivated sellers and buyers. That's just me, though; it can be a good tool to try out as a starting point to build up confidence and learn the market.

Dealers

Getting to know the mobile home dealers in your area will help you gain experience and insight into the business. Dealers work with buyers and sellers of mobile homes every day. They understand the business and have seen changes in the industry throughout the years.

Get to Know the Mobile Home Dealerships in Your Area

Take the time to get to know the dealers in your area. Even better, if there are dealers near the parks you wish to work in it's best to visit them as well. Talk to them and get to know them. Let them get to know you. Do not go in asking for leads. This is a big mistake investors make.

Before you receive, you must give. By giving them information about you and what you do, they will get to know you. This business is about creating relationships. Figure out how you can help them. Maybe as you encounter buyers and sellers from your advertising and experience, you may run into someone who wants to buy a mobile home on land—refer these leads to the dealers you know. Make it a win/win situation for everyone.

How Can You Work Together with Mobile Home Dealers?

Many mobile home dealerships work with sellers who need to sell their existing used mobile home in order to buy their new one. When you help those sellers to sell their home, you, the dealership and the sellers all win. Let dealers know that you prefer to buy in parks, and if they know anyone who is selling a mobile home in a park to let you know first. Sometimes dealers have to pull homes out of parks and move them to their lots to make a deal work. But if they know you buy homes in the parks already set up, this will save them and their sellers both time and money with the moving costs involved. Remember, mobile home dealers are not in the business of holding inventory, they are in the business of selling inventory.

Bring Your Marketing Materials

Go in with a smile and your business cards. Offer to do a presentation for the office regarding what you do.

When I first started out, I learned a lot from mobile home dealers about my area and the history of the mobile home business in the area. I learned about old parks and new parks. The dealers do this every day—they live and breathe mobile homes. I did a couple presentations for a couple of offices, brought in coffee and donuts and got a few leads there. The key is to develop strong relationships so that you are first in their mind when an opportunity comes up.

Again, this may not be the right approach for everyone. If you do not like talking in front of people, this may not be a viable option.

Contractors

Contractors (especially those who do business in the parks and areas where you wish to work) can be a good source of leads and information. These people want your business. Remember, you will be building your team, so even if the contractors you meet don't provide you with leads, it's always good to be on the lookout for new team members.

Networking with Contractors

I would start out by calling contractors who do business and advertise in the parks/areas you wish to work in. Most times, the park managers will have a few contractors they work with on hand, though I've found many good contractors (some even offering lower-cost services) just by picking up their business cards and/or flyers in the parks/areas where I work.

Give them a call. Find out about them. Let them know about you. If these contractors are constantly working on mobile homes, most likely they are in front of mobile home owners all the time. There's a good chance these homeowners will need to sell or know someone who needs to sell down the road. Remember, this business is about relationships. If you can learn to create strong relationships and build rapport with folks, the opportunities are endless.

Working with Other Investors

If you find that you just don't have enough time to dedicate to finding deals on a regular basis, or that negotiating and working with sellers just isn't your cup of tea, working with other investors to help you find opportunities is another route to go. These people look for deals on a regular basis and may actually help you find deals. However, be sure to take the time to learn your market before going this route. Not all investors will have the same standards you do in terms of what you are looking for, so set the parameters yourself.

I meet many investors who say they work with other investors to help them find deals. Whenever I meet people who say this, I ask them their criteria. They usually say, "Just find me a deal and give me the numbers." I would caution that numbers are not everything, and these numbers can be skewed. In most cases, these investors really do not know what they want. Usually, what ends up happening is that they need to confer with other sources to decide whether or not to take action on an opportunity. A serious investor will know how to spot a deal and will make a decision without hesitation. That is why it's very important to really know your market and know what you're looking for.

When it comes to doing deals, you need to do your own due diligence and not rely on others solely for the numbers. If you take the time to learn your market, you'll be able to recognize opportunities. When you know your market, you'll be way ahead of the game.

Working with Banks (Bank-Owned Mobile Homes)

Working with banks on mobile homes they have taken back is another way to find opportunities in this business. Usually, if you have a good relationship with the park managers, you'll get to know these opportunities before anyone else. The park managers will tell you which homes have been taken back by the bank due to unpaid rent. In many cases, the banks may not pay back lot rent and may pass that cost on to the buyer of the mobile home.

In some states, you need to have a dealer's license to buy directly from the bank. If you wish to go this route, check your local housing authority for the laws in your area.

My Experience Working with Banks

Personally, I haven't had much success working with banks. In my experience, they have tried to get every penny they can on the home. One thing I don't like about working with banks is they sell in "as-is" condition. Most times, all the utilities have been turned off, so you don't have the opportunity to test them out. Depending on your comfort level, this can be a good or bad thing. The good is it leaves room for negotiating, but the bad, of course, is that if all the systems aren't working, you'll have to get them fixed later.

Usually in this case, the park manager will know the story on the home, and can let you know whether the home was taken care of or not. Also, you can check with the neighbors. In the past, I've knocked on doors of the neighbors around the home in question, and they have usually told me the condition of the home. I find that many people do know their neighbors in the parks I've chosen to work in.

Another reason I don't like working with banks is that you are dealing with an entity, most likely over the phone. You don't have the chance to build face-to-face rapport unless you can meet with a representative locally. That said, there have been some investors who have been successful working with banks. In fact, for some, this has been their sole source of leads. Again, it will depend on your personality and comfort level. Do what works for you.

Working with Real Estate Agents

Real estate agents can be another source of leads. Just like mobile home dealers, they work with sellers and buyers all the time. When driving parks and/or homes on land, you will find some listed by real estate agents.

Take the time to call the agents and learn more about them and what they do. Try to find someone who has experience specifically working with mobile home sellers and buyers. If you can find an agent who understands what you do, he or she could be a good source of leads for the future.

To be honest, most real estate agents need help when it comes to selling mobile homes—there are not many cash buyers for them out there. If you can help their clients who need to sell their mobile homes, that's good for everyone. If you find an agent who is in front of mobile home sellers frequently, and you have a good rapport with him or her, hopefully this person will think of you when an opportunity arises.

Direct Mail/Door-to-Door Marketing

If you're an organized person, you may want to try direct mail and/or door-to-door marketing to find sellers of mobile homes. I know folks who have gone this route and been successful. Remember, though, that this form of marketing takes a lot of persistence (multiple mailings) and an organized approach.

Personally, I have never done a direct mail campaign for mobile homes. As I've mentioned before, however, I have gone door to door in parks and talked to homeowners while passing out flyers. It has generated interest and helped to get the word out. For me, this is an approach that worked well, but it may not be for everyone.

When It Comes to Marketing, Do What Works for You

So these are a few ways you can market to get the word out and find sellers of mobile homes. Again, choose the methods that are a good fit for you. Do what works best for your personality. Pick just a few of the suggestions above that seem like they would suit you, and try them out. At first, it will be a lot of trial and error, but soon you will get the hang of it and find out what works for you.

Once you get the word out and your marketing gets going, then you will be ready to meet with sellers and start evaluating opportunities.

Chapter 15

Working with Sellers

In the beginning, it may be very overwhelming to talk to and meet with sellers. Many new investors don't really know what to do and how to evaluate opportunities; this is why it's so important to learn your market. But the catch-22 is, in order to learn your market you need to get out there in the field, which involves meeting with sellers.

Talking with Sellers

When you first call sellers on the phone, there are a couple of questions you need to ask. (A full questionnaire is provided in the appendix section of this book.) Usually, the first question I ask sellers is how they heard about me. This will tell you if and where your marketing is coming from. Make note of it, because if you are receiving calls from one marketing method, you will want to continue that method in the future. Continue with activities that work, stop activities that do not work.

While on the phone with sellers, I let them do all the talking. Sure, you want to ask questions, but put them in the driver's seat—let them explain to you their situation, why they are selling and why they have called you.

In this business, I've learned that listening is more important than talking. You can learn a lot just by listening to what the seller is saying and by paying attention to the types of words a seller is using. Don't try to talk over the seller's head or while the seller is talking, and don't talk too much. I see a lot of investors out there who try to make it seem like they are better than the seller; they talk like a professional investor. Sellers don't like that. They want to work with someone they can trust, and someone they can trust will most likely be someone who can relate to and understand their situation.

Why I Present Myself as "Mom and Pop"

When I talk to sellers, I don't try to be a big shot. I tell them I am a local person (notice I don't use the word "investor") looking to buy a mobile home. I stop there. If they ask if I'm an investor, I say I buy mobile homes to rent or to sell on payments because it's hard to find a cash buyer. But I don't use the word "investor"—as I said before, it has a bad connotation to the general public. Most folks understand the explanation I give, and they see me at their level, which is what I want.

This is just my style. There are some investors out there who do take a different approach. They approach sellers with a company and investor mentality—they tell sellers they buy and sell homes as investors, and that they do this all the time.

I'm not going to say this approach does not work. Some people make it work quite well, but in my opinion, most sellers want to work with people they can trust, and I find that most folks feel they can trust a smaller operation and someone they can relate to (like me) over a large operation (and an investor who presents him or herself as rich and different from the seller).

The Advantage of Visiting Sellers

As I've said before, most investors will not go out and visit sellers for several reasons—the asking price is too high, the home is not in a location they desire, etc. Use this to your advantage because even though you may not buy right now, you will accomplish two things by visiting a seller in person. One, you will learn your market by visiting a lot of homes and will learn to evaluate the types of home you like and don't like. And two, if you are the only person who has visited the seller, his or her situation may change in the future (i.e., he or she may lower the price), and the seller will remember you as the one who took the time to go out in person.

Now, I've told you that when I first started out, I met with every single seller I spoke with, even if the home was priced too high, even if it was miles and hours away. That time and effort really paid off because these days, when I receive calls I know the areas and types of homes people are talking about only because of my early experiences visiting these types of opportunities. Had I not taken the time then, I would not know the market as well as I do now.

Meeting with Sellers

The first couple of times you meet with sellers, you will stumble. Do not worry. Do not go in thinking you will buy their home. You are there for the learning experience. Will you buy their home? You're not sure. Why? You still need to learn the market.

When you first meet with a seller, let him or her guide you through the home. Usually, we start with the inside and then work our way to the outside. When I go through homes, I take on a homeowner-type mentality. I do not think like an investor. Why? I do this because I feel that if I am going to buy a home and market it, I need to have a product I can stand behind: a good home. My test for this is if I would live in the home myself. If I can see myself living in the home, then I will pursue the opportunity. If not, then I will pass on it. This is just my style; you might feel comfortable investing in homes in which you would not live.

Chapter 16

Inspecting Mobile Homes

When going through the home, I have the seller guide me, typically from the living room to the kitchen and then the bedrooms and bathrooms. While looking around, I check everything. And I mean everything. I go in just like I am a homeowner looking for a home to buy for myself.

What to Bring When Inspecting Mobile Homes

Be sure to bring a notebook and pen to jot down notes about the home. Write down everything you see as well as what the seller tells you. Remember to take a homeowner mentality and test everything out. I've also learned it's helpful to bring a digital camera to help me remember the homes. Lastly, make sure you also bring a good flashlight and batteries. Sometimes the lighting in the homes can be a bit dim, and you'll want to make sure you see everything. *(Note: There is a questionnaire at the back of this book that will help you when inspecting homes.)*

Ceiling

The first thing I check when entering every room is the ceiling. Be sure to turn on all the lights when inspecting the ceiling, and look at the ceiling in every closet and/or cabinet as well. When I look at the ceiling, I check for any water damage. If you see rings on the ceiling, this is a sign of water damage. Be sure to ask the seller if they have had any water and roof issues in the past.

Living Room

While in the living room, I usually check the floors (make sure they are stable), the walls and around the windows (look for any moisture issues). Turn on and off the lights, look behind and underneath the furniture. Be careful; I was in a living room once in an older home where the floor was unstable. The seller told me a section of the floor was really sensitive and needed to be replaced. When I stepped on it, my foot went right through!

Kitchen and Dining Area

In the kitchen area, I test out the stove and make sure all the burners and oven are working. Usually, the home will have either a gas or electric stove. Then I go to the sink and run the water—I make sure it gets both hot and cold water. I open the cabinet underneath to make sure there are no leaks. If you see a bucket or a pot underneath the sink, this is a sign there is or has been a leak there. If you see a sign of leakage, be sure to bring the issue up to the seller.

I then open up all the cabinets and make sure they are all in good condition. I check the refrigerator and freezer to make sure they are working properly. I feel the floors and make sure they are stable. Some homes will have both a kitchen and dining area—this is a good feature of a home. Make note of it if you visit one that has a separate dining room.

Hallway

The hallway area is usually where the heating unit is stored (if central heat and air) as well as the utility hookups, such as for a washer and dryer, if applicable. Be sure to check the floor, especially if it's carpeted, as a carpet can hide problems. I've been in some hallways that are carpeted only to find soft spots in the floor. Test the heating and air-conditioning unit. Make sure they are both working properly.

Bedrooms

When inspecting bedrooms, the first thing I do is turn on the light, even in the daytime. If the lights are not on, you can miss something. Check all corners of the room and lift up all the furniture. Look under the beds. Check the closets. Be sure to check the ceiling in the closet—this can be an area with a few hidden spots. If it's dark, use your flashlight to check for damage and/or moisture issues.

Look around the windows. Look for any signs of water damage, especially at the ceiling. Again, feel around the floors. Make sure the floors are stable and look for any soft spots.

Bathrooms

Many times a bathroom will be attached to the master bedroom, and another will be off to the side in the hallway by the other bedrooms. When inspecting bathrooms, turn on the lights and look for any moisture problems. Again, windows, ceilings and inside closets are notorious places for moisture problems. Look underneath the sink, run the water and make sure there are no leaks.

Be sure the faucet gets both cold and hot water. Also, check the tub and make sure it's properly draining. Lastly, check the toilet and shower area, if applicable. Flush the toilet to make sure it's working. If there's anything else that could possibly not be working, check it.

Exterior

Once I'm done inspecting the inside of the home, then we move to the outside. When inspecting the outside, be sure the seller is with you as you walk around the exterior of the home because you will want to ask the seller questions here too. I've been in situations where the seller wanted to stay inside while I inspected the outside because it was too hot or cold outside. Try to get the seller to be with you outside as you inspect the home.

Deck/Porch Area

This is the first place I inspect since it's right by the front entrance. Make sure the porch and deck area are stable. Check the railing for stability and moisture issues. If there is an overhang, make sure it's attached properly for safety issues. Ask the seller if the deck/porch will stay when the home is sold.

(Note: It's always important to ask if a particular item will stay with the home. If not, you may be in for a surprise after you purchase it. I've been in many situations where the seller has taken certain items from the home, including the deck/ porch area. It's best not to assume anything.)

Siding

After checking the deck and porch area, I usually walk around the exterior of the home. Take your time, especially during the first couple of homes you inspect. Be sure to take pictures of everything. Go up to the siding of the home and feel for any moisture issues. Usually, the siding will be either aluminum or hardiboard siding (wood/masonite siding). If the siding is aluminum, in most cases there will not be any moisture issues. However, if the siding is hardiboard siding, this may be an issue, so feel around, especially near the bottom of the home below the windows.

Moisture Issues with Hardiboard/Masonite Siding

Hardiboard (masonite/wood) siding needs to be replaced on a regular basis. In most cases, this is due to moisture issues. Be sure to check the top of the home for gutters. When it rains, is the water being directed away from the home? Or is it running down the side? If it's running down the side of the home, this can be problematic and can lead to moisture issues.

Check the siding all the way around the home. Make sure everything is sturdy and in place. Look for water damage and moisture issues. If there are certain areas that have moisture issues and water damage, take note of them. You will have to figure these in as repair costs. It can be a good negotiating point.

Skirting

Be sure to check the skirting around the home. In many cases, the skirting will be vinyl and sometimes will have holes at the bottom due to weed killers/weed eaters. This is OK. Just make sure it's intact. If there is skirting missing, this will need to be addressed and worked into your repair costs. Many parks have a policy that their homes must be completely skirted and covered at all times.

Back of the Home

Check the back of the home again for any damage, especially water and moisture issues. Here you will find the HUD label number, an identification number for the home. It will be a rectangular gray seal on the lower left side of the home (when facing the home). Take note of this number, as it identifies the home. If the home is an older model (i.e., 1980s and older), there may not be a seal. That's OK as long as the seller has the title and any documents to identify the home.

Back Porch/Stairs

Usually, there will be a back door on the other side of the home with a porch or stairs leading from it. Be sure the stairs and porch are stable and secure. Check over the doorway to be sure there are no moisture and water issues. Sometimes if there is no flashing above the door, water can get through and will create moisture issues in the future.

Side of the Home—Air-Conditioning Unit

If there is central air-conditioning (A/C) in the home, most likely the A/C unit will be on the same side of the home as the back porch. Be sure it's intact and in working order. Check the inside of the unit—if it's very rusty outside, this means there could be future issues with it, as water may be getting on the inside. Bring this up with the seller. Be sure to ask how old the unit is and when, if ever, the unit was last serviced and/or replaced.

Hot Water Heater

Depending on the age of the home, this item can be either on the inside (usually in the master bedroom closet behind a screwed-in panel) or outside of the home. While not necessary to look at, I do check the hot water heater to make sure the home is properly receiving hot water in all areas of the home. Be sure to ask the seller the age of the hot water heater. If it's never been replaced and the sellers have owned the home for a long time, be sure to take note of this.

Roof

The roof can be one of the biggest problem areas in a home. Check the outside roof. When inspecting the roof,

I walk as far back as I need to until I can see the roof. Look for any signs of moisture and/or damage.

Usually, if you see any black spots (an indication of mold) or rust spots (if the roof is metal), you will be able to tell that there is moisture damage. Also, check the sides of the roof to make sure there are no moisture issues. Ask the seller when the roof was last resealed, recoated and/or replaced. It's usually best to reseal/recoat a roof every two to three years.

Ask Questions—Lots of Them!

When inspecting homes, I make sure to take my time inspecting and asking questions. In my experience, I've found what matters most is whether the seller seems trustworthy. You will only be able to learn this through experience and by asking him or her lots of questions.

If the seller seems to answer your questions truthfully (you can tell by body language and overall tone), then you will get a true feeling for the home and know of any known issues up front. However, if the seller does not seem trustworthy and you get the feeling he or she is not being honest with you and may be hiding something, chances are you will be mostly on your own to determine the condition of the home.

Chapter 17

Types of Sellers I Choose to Work With

I choose only to work with sellers who are truthful and trustworthy, no matter how good the deal may be. My philosophy is that if I can't trust the seller and/or the person I'm working with, then I'd rather pass on the opportunity. No deal is worth all the hassle and time involved if you can't trust each other—it's just not good business. There are some investors who may do things differently, but I prefer not to risk it.

Determine the Seller's Time Frame

After you take the time to inspect the home, you want to ask the seller a few more questions. One of the most important questions to ask is the person's time frame—when they're thinking of moving and/or selling. Usually, a motivated seller will have a time frame for when they are leaving and want to sell. If the seller does not have a time frame, this is an indication of a less motivated seller—he or she may be just shopping around for offers.

Other Questions to Ask

You'll also want to ask whether the seller has the title to the home. (You should have asked this already on the phone, but ask it again anyway.) If so, can you see it? Also, is the home all electric or gas? How much are the taxes per year? Do they go up and/or down?

Be sure to ask as many questions as you can. This accomplishes two things. First, it gives you the information you need to determine whether this home will be a good investment, and answers questions you would want to know as a potential homeowner. Second, it builds rapport with the seller—it lets him or her know you are not there just to negotiate on price and that's it (as many investors are). It shows that you are truly interested in the home and are trying to determine if it's a good fit for you to create a win/win situation for everyone. Most sellers appreciate this, especially those who have been in the home for quite some time. Remember, you are there to help.

(Note: There is a questionnaire at the back of this book to help you with what to ask of sellers.)

Chapter 18

Negotiating and Making Offers

Once you have inspected the home, you are ready to negotiate with the seller. Again in this step, I let the seller do all the talking while I listen. I ask the seller again about the price she was thinking of selling the home for. Sellers will usually answer with the same price they quoted on the phone, or lower. Then I tell the seller all the repairs needed, and ask her what the price would be if she wanted to sell "as-is" with no repairs and her closing costs covered. She'll quote a price. Then I ask, "What if this were all cash?" Also ask whether she was planning on taking only cash or taking payments. Some sellers name a cash price, while others say it's the same price either way.

Depending on what the seller says and her motivation level, I will either tell her I'll have to think about it and get back to her (if the price is too far from my target price) or ask her if there is some way we could try to work together, maybe work something out that works for both of us. If the seller says, "No, this is my final price," and is firm on it, then I know this seller is not as motivated as I prefer to work with. I thank her for her time and say I'll have to think about it and will touch base again in a few weeks. On the other hand, if the seller says, "Sure, we can work something out. I really need to sell," then I proceed with negotiations.

Again, it's really important to learn your market. Know the value of the home (i.e., wholesale, retail, owner finance, etc.) before you go into the appointment. If it's your first time in, it's best to go with the numbers the park manager has given you.

Negotiating Takes Practice and Time

Negotiating is more an art than a science. It will take practice. Over time, you will learn (as I have) how to get a feel for the seller and his motivation. It's a game—a game of how to come to an agreement and create a win/win situation for everyone. In the beginning, you will stumble, but as you meet more and more sellers, you will improve through experience. Believe me, I did.

Figuring in Repairs

If there are repairs to be made to the home and you are not quite sure of their costs, ask the seller what he thinks it would cost to make the repairs. Sometimes he will give you a figure, sometimes he won't. If he doesn't know, ask the seller if you can bring a few contractors by to quote you the repair costs and ask if he would be willing to deduct the repair costs (within reason, of course) from the price of the home. In most cases, if the seller is motivated enough he will agree to this.

Now, this is just one technique I use. If the seller starts quoting prices for repairs and you're comfortable with them, then you can go straight into negotiations and try to come to a price for the home that you are both comfortable with.

How I Negotiate

Negotiations tend to require a lot of back and forth. This builds both rapport and trust between me and the seller. Now, some investors may be scared that if they don't get the home under contract right away, someone else may.

In my experience, though, what matters most is trust. If the seller truly trusts you and sees your intentions are serious, she will work with you. I've been in so many situations in which I was not the only one talking with the seller. However, the seller trusted me more than anyone else and eventually we worked together. Above all else, the relationship is what counts. A piece of paper means nothing without someone's word behind it.

Structuring Your Offers

There are so many ways to structure your offers. The way you choose will depend on your personal comfort level. I do not do much creative financing in my business. Yes, there have been a few cases in which I've had the opportunity to do some creative financing, but I'd much rather buy homes in cash and not have to owe anything to anyone—it's just easier that way. Everyone will have their own style of doing things, though, and what works for me may not work for you.

What Will Stay/Not Stay?

When negotiating a price for the home, you will need to determine what will and will not stay with the home after it's sold. Be sure to ask the seller what he is planning to take with him (e.g., stove, refrigerator, washer and dryer, curtains, etc.). This is very important, as you do not want to be surprised on closing day. If the seller is planning to take some items with him, use this as a negotiating tool. Offer to deduct the cost of the item(s) from the agreed purchase price of the home.

Figure in Repairs with Your Offer

As I mentioned earlier, you'll also want to figure in the repairs needed for the home. I use this as a negotiating tool in many of my deals. Most sellers who need to sell quickly do not want to go back and make repairs to the home— they don't have the time or in most cases, the money. Use this as a negotiating tool.

Closing Costs

As with all real estate transactions, there will be closing costs involved when purchasing mobile homes. Ask the seller how she wants to handle this. (Remember, do more listening than talking.) In most cases, sellers do not want to have any money come out of pocket. This includes bringing money to the closing table. If they are wary of closing costs, offer to pay the closing costs, but deduct the amount from the purchase price. Many sellers will agree to this.

Taxes

Be sure to do all research on taxes owed on the home, and make sure they are paid off. In some locales, you cannot transfer title to mobile homes as personal property without having taxes paid. Furthermore, there are some areas in which the taxes for the following year have to be paid in advance before closing. Be prepared for this and research how this is handled with your local housing authority in advance. You can either prorate the taxes (as in most real estate transactions) or offer to pay the taxes owed and deduct them from the purchase price at closing. It's up to you how you want to handle this issue. Either way, the taxes will need to be paid before closing.

Do Your Research

Before closing on a home, be sure to do your research. Be sure you are talking to the owner of the home, as evidenced by the title. Check that the home is clear of all liens and that taxes are paid. In some areas, you can check the status of the title just by calling the local housing authority. Also, in some locales this can be verified online. Again, it's very important to familiarize yourself with your local housing authority and know how these issues are handled in your area.

Insurance

Make sure the home is covered by insurance on the day of closing. Some investors skimp on insurance because they think nothing bad will happen. But as Murphy's Law attests, "What can go wrong, will go wrong." I always make sure to get insurance on the home starting the day of closing. Usually, I will let my insurance company know beforehand the day we plan to close and set insurance to cover and bind starting that day.

Closing and Possession Date

The closing and the possession date are two very important terms to understand and keep in mind. The closing date is the day the property is transferred officially from the seller to the buyer, on paper. This means that both the buyer and the seller have done all the necessary paperwork to transfer the title. However, the buyer may not necessarily have access to the home on that day. It is the possession date that will determine when the buyer can occupy the home and when the seller must vacate the home. Both of these dates should be reflected in the contract. In most cases, I make the closing and possession date the same day. I tell sellers up front that we cannot close until they are completely moved out of the home. As a rule, I don't like to close on homes with sellers still living in them. This creates too many issues and problems. My belief is that if I buy a home, then I should be able to move into it that day.

Now, I have had a few cases in which the sellers have continued to live in the home after closing, and these were special circumstances. In these cases, I only gave enough funds up front for them to go out and find a new place and/or for moving costs before closing. Then, the rest of the funds were distributed to them once they had completely moved out of the home. Again, this is a judgment call. Do what you feel comfortable doing.

Lot Rent

Be sure to include lot rent in your negotiations. Figure in the time needed for marketing to find a qualified buyer. If you are planning to close at the end of the month, see if you can factor in a month or two of lot rent with the seller and deduct that from the purchase price. In the past, I've been able to do this with some sellers, depending on their motivation level. Again, you want to make sure the lot rent is current—that will be the stipulation in the contract. Also, if you are planning to keep the home where it is (if in a park or on a lot), be sure to cite this in your contract as well.

Contracts

I highly recommend using a contract you feel comfortable with. The contract should be very easy to read and straightforward. Be sure that it conforms to the local laws in your area. There are several books you can reference that have sample mobile home purchase agreements in them (see the Appendix section at the end of this book for some good ones). I would take the time to check these out and note the differences between different contracts. If you plan to use one of these contracts, I suggest having it looked over by an attorney in your area first, and making sure it conforms to local laws.

Once you have worked out all the details on the sale,

the next step is to put it in writing. Be sure to bring two blank contracts with you, one for you and one for the seller. (I don't usually take the time to go make a copy after we fill the contract out—I like to do it right there and just make another one by hand after we do the first one.) The contract ensures that you and the seller are on the same page about everything involved in the sale, and will protect you if problems come up, so take this step seriously.

Chapter 19

Closing and Final Inspection

In most cases, you will not need a title company to close on mobile home sales if you're buying the home as personal property (i.e., no land included). You can use a title company if you choose to, but I don't. Usually, the seller and I will just go to the local housing authority together and submit the necessary paperwork. Beforehand, I call the housing authority to verify what we need for closing. Usually, this involves filling out the proper forms and supplying the housing authority with the documents needed for the title transfer. They will tell you what is needed and the associated fees (if any). This takes only a quick phone call, and all you need is the identification number of the home. Also, in many areas you can look up a home online to verify the title and see what (if any) liens exist on the home.

If there is a lien on the home, there will most likely be paperwork needed to take the lien off. It must be signed and completed by the lien holder. Check on this before closing so everything is taken care of. I've been in situations where sellers still have the title to the home, but the lien has not been taken off. Usually, taking it off involves nothing more than one extra step—submitting a piece of paper and a filing fee to the local housing authority. I've done this with sellers at closing, and it's worked out fine.

On the day of closing, I do a final inspection and walk-through of the home. This is stated in my contract with the seller. Usually, we meet at the home, I do the inspection, and then we go together to the housing office for the closing. The reason I do a final inspection on the day of closing is to be extra sure that everything is as it should be. I want to verify that the home is in the same condition (or better) as when I agreed to purchase the home. In other words, I want to make sure I know what I'm buying.

I make sure everything is in place and matches the terms listed in the contract. If there are any appliances that the contract says should stay, I make sure they are there. Sometimes you'll be surprised at what you find. In one case, the seller actually took the lightbulbs out of the light fixtures in the bathrooms. I was really upset. He told me this was not in the contract, so those lightbulbs were his. Now I am extra careful when filling out contracts and state explicitly what stays and what does not stay. I advise you to do the same.

Attending the Closing

After going through the home and making sure everything is in order, the seller(s) and I lock up the home and leave for the closing together. My philosophy is that once it's closed, the seller gets his funds that day, and I get the keys to the home. That's it. Also, there are no returns. I've had sellers who have asked me, "What if we change our minds after we close? Can we get the house back?" I gently tell them no, that they need to be sure they really want to sell the home before we go any further. You may be laughing, but this happens. Seriously, I'm not a retail store.

Closing Paperwork

At the back of this book, I've made a list of the most common closing paperwork documents I use. Since every area is different, I highly recommend checking local laws (check with your local housing authority) as to the documents needed for closing a mobile home as personal property in your area.

As for the documents themselves, there are many mobile home books and other resources out there that include sample documents. My recommendation is to take these documents as a blueprint and have an attorney look at them and make any revisions to conform to the laws in your area.

Notarizing Documents

One important document I always use is a Bill of Sale. The Bill of Sale is like a receipt to show that you purchased the home from the seller on a certain date. I always notarize the Bill of Sale. The reason I get it notarized is if down the road a problem comes up with the title and the seller is not reachable, then I have evidence that the seller sold me the home.

In my area, this evidence is enough to clear up any title issues where the seller is concerned. However, the Bill of Sale is not the same thing as the title. Remember that. Some sellers will tell you it's the same thing (on the buying end). There have been many sellers who have tried to sell me a home without having title to it—they only have a Bill of Sale. No title, no deal.

Proving Ownership

Checking the title to prove ownership involves one of two things, depending on your area. In some areas, the seller will have a physical title, while in others, the information is logged into a computer. Remember, just because a seller has a Bill of Sale does not mean she has title to the home. In most cases, if you have the serial number or identification number of the home you will be able to check with your local housing authority as to who is on the title. Otherwise, you will need to see a physical title.

If the seller has only a Bill of Sale, he will need to complete the title transfer paperwork with your local housing authority to be able to sell the home properly. Sometimes a seller will only have a Bill of Sale if the prior owner did not have a title either, and if taxes have not been paid. In these cases, I gently tell the seller I cannot buy the home without a clear title to it. It's that simple. Either he takes the extra steps to clear up the title issues, or he tries to sell it to someone who does not care about title issues. I will not buy a home that does not have a clear title to it.

Chapter 20

After the Closing

Once the home is closed, I make preparations to get it ready to go on the market. I personally do not sell in "as-is" condition. I get the home ready to live in before showing it to any potential buyers. I do not put a sign in the window until it's ready to show. In the past, I've put up a sign before the home was ready to sell, and it's caused problems. In one case, my cleaning crew was cleaning a home with a sign in the window, and people kept coming in and out while they were working, interrupting them and asking questions. My cleaning crew was constantly calling me saying there were folks there with questions. It was a hassle for everyone, and they were not able to get their work done efficiently. I learned from this experience never to put a sign in the window until the home is ready to show.

Selling "As-Is" versus Fixing Up

There are some investors who sell in "as-is" condition rather than fixing up a mobile home first. This will be a personal choice on your part. I do not sell "as-is" because

I want to attract the best clientele for the home. That is just my personality and preference.

If you do sell "as-is," be prepared for the fact that you will be limiting your market and attracting a different type of buyer—those who are handy and can do fix-up work. I find in the retail market, most folks want something already fixed up. I have tried the "as-is" route before, but it's been a bit of a nightmare showing homes in "as-is" condition, as many people kept asking if this or that was going to be fixed. Also, many of those willing to buy in "as-is" condition struck me as a bit shady in character. As a result, I've chosen to spend the extra time and money for the homes I buy to be in presentable condition.

Fixing up the Home

Depending on your comfort level and plans for the home, fixing up the home can definitely make a difference in attracting more high-end clientele. One of the most important aspects to selling a home is curb appeal. If the home does not have curb appeal, people will not take the time to see the inside of the home. What I do is compare the home to all the other homes in the neighborhood, and make sure it blends in. The worst thing to do is try to sell the ugliest home on the block. You'll get the best deal on the buying end, but have a hard time selling it.

Outside of the Home

Start with the aesthetics of the home itself—make sure it has a clean look. It is very important for the home to have curb appeal. I cannot stress this enough. For example, if the color of the siding or deck is fading, make a note of it. You may have to paint it. Then, move to the property. If there are leaves, weeds, tall grass, etc., I do a bit of landscaping. These are all cosmetic issues, but create a world of difference in making a home attractive to prospective buyers.

Inside the Home

On the inside, the home must be cleaned from top to bottom. If your budget is tight, you may have to do the cleaning yourself. I did this in the beginning. Most homes require only light cleaning. For heavy cleaning jobs, you'll almost always need to bring in a professional cleaning company. Homes that have had smokers or pets are notorious for needing a professional touch.

There are two parts to cleaning a mobile home—cleaning the floor, and cleaning the rest of the home. Several cleaning companies have told me the floor is one of the most important aspects, and can really make or break the aesthetics of a home. If the floor is dirty, take the time to clean it well—it makes a world of difference. If there are heavy carpet stains on the floor, bring in a professional carpet cleaning company to do the job.

Most Important Areas to Clean

The most important rooms in the home are the living room, kitchen and bathrooms. In my experience, homeowners spend a lot of time in these rooms, and most folks will spend most of their time inspecting these areas as well. Usually, potential buyers just glance at the bedrooms. Many people, especially women, open up all the kitchen cabinets, the stove and the refrigerator, so I make sure these areas are extra clean, especially the appliances. I have included a checklist in the back of this book of the most important items to clean before putting a home on the market. I hope it will help if you decide to go the "fix-up" route.

Chapter 21

Finding Buyers

Once the home is ready to be put on the market, it's time to start marketing it to potential buyers. While there are many ways to market a home, there are only a few that are effective. I've tried many different methods in the past, and the following are the methods I've found to be most effective.

Sign in the Window

Placing a sign in the window of a mobile home is one of the first and best strategies I use when marketing homes. Quite honestly, the people who are the most interested in your home may be people right there living in the park, or their friends and relatives.

Park Manager

The next best way to market is to network with the manager of the park your home is in. The park manager is the gatekeeper of the park—he or she knows what is going on. When folks call, he or she takes the calls. When folks come into the park, whom do they see and talk to? The park manager. In most cases, prospective buyers/tenants make the park office their first stop before they drive through the park. They ask the park manager what he or she has on the market in the park. If you have a good relationship with the park manager, your home will be mentioned and the park manager will direct them to your home.

Signs near the Park

Another effective method I've used in generating interest in homes I have available is placing signs at intersections near the park. Since yours is a local business, it is local folks who will most likely be interested in your home. If you decide to go this route, be sure to check the laws in your area regarding signs. As discussed previously, sometimes you may be able to put signs out on the weekends (near garage sale signs) and then take them down before the start of the week.

Flyers on Local Bulletin Boards near the Park

In the past, I've posted flyers on local bulletin boards near the park. I go to many of the same type of locations where I've advertised that I buy mobile homes, as discussed earlier in this book—gas stations, libraries, Laundromats, grocery stores, etc.

A Word about Marketing

In order to get the greatest return on my investment, I focus my marketing efforts as close as possible to the park where I'm selling a particular mobile home. The reason for this is that most folks who will be interested in the home are those who live locally. And by locally I mean those who live really close to the park. These folks may live just down the street in an apartment or duplex, or they may live a few miles from the park. If you start to market further away from the park than a few miles, you will get potential buyers/tenants who will call, but may be interested in living in another part of town—the part of town you're marketing in.

Chapter 22

Screening Buyers

Once you have your marketing efforts in place, the calls will start to come in. If you are just starting out, I highly recommend you take every single call and meet with as many qualified buyers as possible. Why? As with meeting sellers, it's good practice. Forget about what you hear about automating processes and saving time. In a business, you need to learn the operations firsthand. That means living and breathing each area of your operations.

I did this in the beginning. I answered every call personally and met with as many qualified buyers as I could. This experience taught me a lot. It taught me how to screen people, and it taught me the different behaviors and different types of buyers out there. It taught me what buyers looked for in a home. All in all, it was a very good, educational learning experience. Though it seemed like a lot of work answering so many calls and meeting with so many different people, it was worth it in the end.

Qualifying Buyers

So how do you qualify buyers on the phone? It's really more of an art than an exact science. When buyers call, they will be asking you many of the same questions. You'll need to learn how to be a good listener. Listen not only to what they say, but more importantly, to how they say it. *(Note: In the back of this book, you'll find a script of questions to ask potential buyers.)*

The Most Frequently Asked Questions

After asking questions about the home, most folks who call in will ask you, "How much down and how much per month?" Now, it will be your decision how to answer this question—there are two schools of thought on the issue. *(Note: Be sure to have two prices in mind when sellers call—the cash price and the owner finance price.)*

Your first option is to turn the question around and ask the caller, "How much money do you have for a down payment and how much can you afford per month?" The thinking here is that the people calling in may have more than what you're asking for, and you may shortchange yourself if you give a figure.

Your other option is to go ahead and answer the question. In this case, you already know the market for a down payment and monthly payment, so it will be a standard figure across the board.

Personally, I've done it both ways, but I prefer the second method. In my experience, when I've asked folks how much they can afford to put down and how much they can afford to pay per month, they just ask me, "Well, how much is it?" I think that as consumers, we just want to know the price. I've modeled my negotiations with buyers on what the parks I work with do on their own deals. They don't play games. They tell prospective buyers/tenants exactly how much down and how much per month. I've learned that if I'm in line with their figures, then it's not an issue.

It's up to you which route you want to go. I would say, go with what you're comfortable with. You may want to try both routes to see what works for you.

Don't Be Greedy

I've learned not to be greedy in this business. There have been times when I've gone the greedy route and it's hurt me in the end. Sometimes I've asked for too much money up front with inventory I had available, when the park managers had told me what I could realistically expect to receive. I thought I knew better, only to find out they were right. In the end, this cost me both time and money. From this experience, I've learned it's much better to follow the demands of the market and what the market will bear than to be greedy, thinking I can change it. I know there will always be a market if I offer fair terms on a nice home in a nice park. Always.

Chapter 23

Meeting with Buyers

When a potential buyer calls, I decide on the phone whether or not to meet with him. Before I meet a potential buyer, I make sure he's done a drive-by of the home already. If he has not even driven by the home, I tell him he must drive by before I will go out to meet him.

Now, how do I determine which buyers are serious and which are not? To tell you the truth, it takes practice—lots of practice. These days, I can usually tell right away over the phone whether the folks I'm talking with are serious. Those who are not serious may not sound so motivated and familiar with the area on the phone. For example, they will not be as flexible when it comes to seeing the home and may not know the amenities in the area. They may ask you to show the home when it's more convenient for them, not when it's convenient for you. Also, they will probably ask you questions about the area, such as what schools, gas stations, grocery stores, etc., are nearby. In my experience, usually these people are just looking. People who are serious usually know the area and are familiar with the amenities already. In fact, many I have encountered in the past have told me they have been looking in the area for quite some time, and some go so far as to say they have been looking in the particular park where the home sits. These folks take action and know what they want. Those who are not serious do not take action.

After I qualify a potential buyer on the phone, I make her jump through a few hoops. I don't schedule the appointment right away on the phone. My philosophy is if they are really interested in the home, they will pursue it. If they're not that interested, they won't. This prevents me from wasting my time on buyers who will never end up buying.

I tell the buyer to call me either midweek or at the end of the week to schedule a time to see the home. I ask her what her general schedule is. Often, after telling me their schedule, those who are most interested will say they can meet whenever it is convenient for me when they are not working. This is a tip-off that a person truly is motivated to buy. Those who say they have to check their schedule and see what works for them are usually the ones who just want to look at the home.

Serious Buyers versus "Lookie Lous"

For me, serious buyers take priority over the "Lookie Lous." Most times, the serious buyers already know they want to live in the area in which I'm selling. They tell me things like they've been looking there for a long time, their kids go to school in the same school district, they work in the area, etc. When I hear these types of statements, I know these are serious buyers. On the other hand, the not-so-serious buyers (aka the "Lookie Lous") ask me about what types of establishments are close by, where the grocery store and gas station are, and what school district the home is in. These types of questions are a red flag that these folks haven't done their homework and are not as serious.

Serious buyers know they want to live in the area where you're selling. They already know the types of amenities and establishments in the area. Serious buyers are the ones I choose to work with.

Meeting with Serious Buyers

OK, you're out of the stage where you're meeting with all potential buyers for the experience. You've found buyers you've determined are serious. Now it's time to start setting up appointments with them. Again, make them jump a few hoops. Have them call you back on a certain day and/or time to set up the appointment. Put yourself in the driver's seat, not the other way around.

I always arrive at least thirty minutes early when meeting with potential buyers to make sure everything is set up the way I want it to be. If the home has been closed up for awhile, open up the windows and let the air circulate. If you have air freshener, bring it and use it.

When the buyers arrive, take them inside. I let them walk around the home and tell them to feel free to ask any questions they may have. Sometimes while they go through, I take the time to explain the features of the home. Usually, I go into the utilities—is it gas or electric, or both. Also, we talk about the local area a lot. Most times, I just try to build rapport with potential buyers to get a feel for them. If I see it as a good fit, then I make a note of it.

After viewing the home, the buyers will tell you one of two things. Most people will say they have to think about it. The really serious ones will ask about the application process. If it gets to the application process, most times I say there are two applications—one for the home (my application) and another for the park. I tell them they have to pass both. And it's just like applying for an apartment; the park manager and I both check three main things: landlord history, job and criminal history.

If they are truly serious, they will take both applications (I usually keep both of them in the home) and fill them out. A lot of times, they ask if there's anyone else applying. Usually there is, and I tell them that yes, there have been some other interested parties. Then I say that if everything checks out, there's a good chance they may get the home. This gives them incentive to get the application in quickly.

The park will usually charge an application fee. Personally, I don't charge an application fee because I don't feel it's necessary. However, some mobile home sellers do, and it's an individual choice.

Chapter 24

Going over Buyer Applications

To screen buyers, I collect my own applications and do my own due diligence. Yes, there is a park application and the park has its own, similar screening process, but I find it good practice to protect myself by adding another layer of due diligence—my own. If this is going to be a long-term relationship, I want to make sure I really know the folks I'm working with.

As I mentioned above, there are three main aspects I verify when going over applications:

1. Job

2. Landlord history

3. Criminal history

Job

First, I make sure the applicant has at least three times the amount of money coming in (gross) per month as will be required for my monthly payment. This is a minimum standard. If not, the person is not qualified to pay for the home. For example, if the monthly payment for the home (including the lot rent) is $1,000, I make sure the person's gross monthly income is at least $3,000.

Most times, I verify this amount with either the prospective buyer's Human Resources department or her supervisor(s). Most times, you will need authorization from the prospective buyers to release this information. I include this in the application. I just fax over the application to their employer along with a cover sheet and usually we're good to go.

Now, if the prospective buyer just started a job or is new in town, be really careful. Most times, the parks I work with require a steady work history. If it looks like the prospective buyer is hopping around from job to job in a short period of time, that shows instability. Many of the buyers I've chosen to work with have a stable work history—they've been at their current job for a couple of years already.

On the other hand, there will be circumstances in which people are new to town and pick up a job in the same industry as they were working in before. Quite honestly, this situation is a bit rare in my experience among those looking for mobile homes. But when it does happen, I find the most qualified are those who grew up in the area and have come back after living elsewhere. Those who are brand new to the area are often less qualified, as they are still making a decision about whether to live there and exactly where.

Landlord History

The next thing I check is the person's landlord payment history. In most cases, folks I've worked with are coming from apartments. Typically, they have already been through a screening process to live there. In most cases, if there has been a steady payment history with few to no late payments and no evictions, then they are qualified for my home. On the other hand, if there is a pattern of late payments or even evictions, that is a red flag, and they are put at the bottom of the pile.

Be careful about those who say they have been living with relatives. In my experience, I find these people to be the least qualified. Usually, these folks have never been on their own and may not have had experience with the responsibility of managing household finances. Many parks will want to see a stable history of landlord payments. Without a history of landlord payments, it may be difficult for some folks to qualify in these parks.

When I first started in the mobile home business, a manager of a high-end park told me she had been trained to verify the landlord history first. In her experience, she told me, if the person has a good landlord history, then the rest of the application should check out. I've taken her advice ever since, and it's worked.

Criminal

This one is self-explanatory. Usually if an applicant has a criminal history, he or she does not pass. Most of the parks I work with will not allow folks with criminal histories to live there.

Evictions and Foreclosures/Bankruptcy

Most parks I work with will not pass those who have been through evictions. Again, I tend to work in high-end parks, which have stricter criteria than other types of parks. Regarding foreclosure and bankruptcy, usually this is looked at on a case-by-case basis. Other factors that are considered include time elapsed since foreclosure/bankruptcy, job situation, etc.

Evaluating Buyers

When evaluating prospective buyers, the decision comes down to two things:

1.   Do they pass the application?

2.   Are they easy to work with?

Remember, you will be entering into a long-term relationship with these people if you decide to work with them and finance/lease option the home. It is your decision whether or not you want to work with them.

In my experience, I've learned not to be so eager to accept the first application that comes through. I tell folks who are interested they will need to fill out an application with me and with the park, but there are also others who may be interested.

When evaluating buyers, you will get a "feeling" for those who are easy to work with versus not easy to work with. Those who are easy to work with will be able to follow your instructions in applying for the home and will be less demanding. Those who are not, may not follow instructions and may be more demanding. It takes time and practice to get a feel for people, but after awhile you'll get the hang of it.

(Note: In the back of this book, I provide a worksheet for evaluating buyers.)

Chapter 25

Choosing Your Buyers

When choosing buyers, I'm very careful about whom I work with. There are many ways I can tell whether or not I want to work with a certain buyer. One of the ways is when I first talk with her on the phone. If she seems a bit demanding even before I meet her and/or asks certain questions (e.g., what if I pay late?), that is a red flag.

Even moreso, I can tell a lot about buyers when they go through the home. This is why it's so important (in my opinion) in the beginning to take calls and meet prospective buyers. Going through the home(s) with prospective buyers has taught me a lot about screening because I am there and see firsthand the types of issues that concern them.

When going through the home with prospective buyers, if they make a big deal about little things (like a small speck of dirt) or ask if certain little things can be fixed up or painted (maybe they don't like the wall being white), then I know they are high-maintenance buyers. On the other hand, if they go through the home and generally like it and don't ask for many things to be fixed up, they are potential candidates. What I look for are qualified buyers who are low-maintenance and will not be difficult to work with.

Of course, this takes a bit of practice. I remember my first couple of deals. I was constantly answering the phone, screening buyers and meeting potential buyers at the homes. At first, it was a lot of work. I was very overwhelmed. But after awhile it became second nature to me—I gained a lot of experience and learned a lot just by taking the time to screen buyers on the phone and meet them in person myself.

My philosophy is that if I'm going to be in a long-term relationship with these folks, I'd better make sure they are 100 percent qualified and easy to work with.

Once you have chosen your buyers, then you can set a date for the closing. The closing paperwork is all very simple. Many mobile home books and courses offer samples of this paperwork; see the Appendix for recommendations.

Notarizing Closing Documents

Personally, I do notarize my documents. I know this is an extra step and may require an extra fee, but I want the peace of mind of knowing that if any issues should ever come up, then the signature(s) on the documents were verified and confirmed by a third party—the notary.

Often, your bank will notarize your documents for you for free. On the weekends, there are a few banks that are open extended hours and can do this as well. Otherwise, I've done closings during buyers' lunch hours, and it's worked out fine.

(Note: In the back of this book, I provide a checklist of the documents I use for my closings. Sample documents can be found in other mobile home books and courses.)

What I Do That Sets Me Apart from the Competition

I choose to offer buyers a sixty-day habitability warranty on the home. This means that for two months after their purchase, I will warrant that the home is habitable. If any of the major systems—A/C, electrical, plumbing, etc.—do not work and render the home uninhabitable, then I will fix those items. This is one policy that has set me apart from the competition. People get peace of mind from knowing the home they are buying has a warranty. We do a walk-through of the home before we close, and if something needs fixing under the terms of the warranty, I tell them to send it to me in writing.

Who Pays Lot Rent?

Once you have closed on the home, the buyers can move in. I make the buyers responsible for paying lot rent. I do not collect lot rent from the buyers—they pay the park directly. The buyers do all the necessary paperwork with the park. By making buyers responsible for paying the lot rent, it gives them more of a homeowner type of mentality. If for some reason the lot rent does not get paid, I request that the park manager notify me immediately. If the buyers fall really behind on the lot rent and the park is forced to file for eviction, I have an arrangement with the park that I will cover the back lot rent owed, though this has never happened. This gives the park assurance and peace of mind that if buyers ever fall behind on lot rent, it would be paid either way. Most of the parks I work with have very strict screening criteria, and the folks they allow to live in the park are responsible. That is why it's so important for me to work only in the best parks. In my experience, I find the best parks attract the best types of buyers—those who pay.

Chapter 26

Taking Back a Mobile Home: What if They Stop Paying?

As a prior landlord, I have faced this question—what if they stop paying? This is a big hurdle for those who are thinking about getting into mobile home investing. As with all investments, there are risks involved. The key is learning how to manage risk.

Homeowners' versus Renters' Mentality

There is a difference between homeowners and renters, and it's an important difference to remember when trying to pick the right buyers—you want the ones with a homeowner-type mentality, not a renter-type mentality.

In general, most homeowners do not want to lose their home. On the other hand, those who are renters may not care. The trick is to make sure you pick folks who have a homeowner mentality—make sure the folks you work with really do want a place to call their own, not just a place where they can live while trying to squeeze every penny out of you.

If you decide to offer owner financing with the mobile homes you purchase, you really need to put yourself in the shoes of a lender. Be careful whom you choose.

Steps to Take if They Stop Paying

If, despite your having chosen wisely, your buyers stop paying, the first thing I do is give them a phone call. It really doesn't matter what time of the day I call. If I have a good relationship with my buyers, they take my calls. If I get voice mail, I leave a message for them to call me back. I give them one day to call.

If I do not receive a call back in one day, the next step I do is post a notice. I learned this trick from the park managers—this is what the parks do. The notice says the payment has not been received, and that payment must be sent in ASAP to avoid further action. Then it says to contact the property manager (me) and is signed.

When it comes to working with buyers, I play the good guy. I'm on their side. I make a divide between me and my business, just like the park managers do. I act like an employee of my company—the buyers and I are still on good terms, and I'm just doing my job. If the buyers have an issue with making payments, I tell them the procedures of the company.

Now, some investors get a little personal when it comes to working their business. I know of some investors who prefer to have a one-on-one, owner-to-buyer relationship. If there's an issue, they try to work it out among themselves—which is OK if it works for them. Personally, I don't like going that route. I prefer just to act as an employee of the company, the property manager. The model I've taken is from the parks themselves. I see the park managers deal with day-to-day issues all the time. Those who treat it like a business are successful, so I have emulated their model.

If there's a problem with payment, I talk to the buyers as a representative of my company. I make it clear that any requests to the company must be made in writing. Sometimes there are folks who try to push the limit. Well, it's hard to push the limit against a company—it's much easier to do so against an individual.

Usually when I post a notice on a nonpaying buyer's door, the buyer calls me back right away. In my experience, most times this has happened it's been a case of the payment getting lost in the mail. I know some people will think this is an excuse, but it does happen. I train folks always to keep proof of payment, whether it be the receipt or stub for the money order or the cashier's check. They send that to me if this is the case.

Taking Further Action

If after posting a notice I don't get a phone call back, then I know it's time to take further action. If you sold on owner financing, this means taking the next steps toward filing for foreclosure. If you sold on rent to own, this means filing for eviction.

Personally, I've never had to file for eviction or foreclosure in this business. I've been careful to choose the right types of buyers from the outset—those who have a homeowner mentality and who seem trustworthy and hardworking—in order to prevent these sorts of issues.

My Experience Taking a Home Back

I have, however, had to take a home back—luckily only once, though. It was a couple who had informed me they wanted to move out on land. We sat down one day to go over their options. I told them they still had quite a large balance, and could try to sell if they wanted. Otherwise, I'd just have to take the home back, but would request they leave it in clean condition.

They chose to move out quietly, and they left the home in great condition. Since they had a homeowner-type mentality, they had even done a few upgrades to the home.

Within a short time frame after they moved out, I got

the home cleaned up and ready to market, and found a nice family right away to move in. It went very smoothly.

So yes, there are times when not everything works out as planned, and there is always the possibility of having to take a mobile home back. The important thing is learning how to find the right buyers for your home to prevent problems from arising in the first place.

Chapter 27

Record Keeping

To make record keeping easy, I make a file for every home that I buy. This file contains two folders: the seller paperwork and the buyer paperwork. The seller file contains every document and correspondence with the person(s) who sold me the home, as well as forwarding information, such as an address and telephone number. Be sure to have this information on hand, as issues may come up. I remember on one home I bought, I had to have the water heater checked out after the fact, and I wasn't sure if it ran on electric or gas, or where in the home it was located. Since I kept the seller's contact information, I was able to give the seller a call to ask. The seller told me what I needed to know, and told me to call with any other questions.

This is why it's important to maintain good relationships with people—if you take care of others, they will take care of you.

The buyer file contains every document and correspondence I've had with the buyers of the home. I also make a copy of every single payment they make to me, and document every single conversation we have.

Requests for Receipts in Writing

Some have asked whether I print out statements and issue receipts to buyers for every payment they make. Since this sort of administrative task can become a bit tedious, I only do this upon request, and this request must be made in writing.

I've had a couple of buyers who have requested this, and I do issue them receipts every month. For the most part, though, as long as the buyers and I have a relationship built on trust, it's not a big deal for them not to get a receipt. I tell them they can always contact me should they want to know what they owe on the home. Again, this request must be done in writing.

As for record-keeping software, it's really a personal choice. I do recommend, however, that you have some type of software and a system for keeping records. Personally, I choose to have a physical folder filing system as well as digital records on the computer.

The way you choose to keep track of your correspondence with buyers and sellers is also a personal decision. Whether you use a digital or a physical system will be up to you. I've done both—physically written notes and kept digital versions. Whichever method you choose, be sure to record the date and time of your conversation, the person's phone number, whether it was an inbound or outbound call and the nature of the call.

Chapter 28

After the First Deal

Once you've done your first deal, it's time to go out and celebrate. Congratulations! By doing your first deal, you have experienced what it's really like to invest in mobile homes.

After you complete your first deal, I highly recommend you write down your experience with the deal and take some time to reflect. What did you learn? What obstacles did you face? Did things go according to plan, or did you encounter the unexpected? If you did, how did you handle it?

Keeping a Mobile Home Journal

I keep a mobile home journal, in which I write down my experiences and take the time to reflect on these experiences and what I've learned. It's a good exercise. I do visit past entries from time to time to reflect on the earlier days and how things have changed. Reading what I've written in the past can sure bring back memories. It also reminds me of what I've learned and may give me ideas for future deals.

Once you've done your first deal, you can decide whether this business is for you. Only after you've completed your first deal will you fully understand what's involved. From there, you can decide whether or not you would like to continue with the mobile home business.

This business is not for everyone. I have known some investors who try this business out and do a deal or two, only to find out it's not for them. Again, it's all a matter of preference and personality.

The nice thing about this business is that you can get into a deal for a fairly small amount of money, as compared to other forms of real estate investing (e.g., single family homes, apartment buildings, etc.). Plus, if you find you don't want to continue in this business but still have a mortgage note in place, you can always sell your note to another investor. That's the beauty of mobile home investing.

Chapter 29

Why I Enjoy Mobile Home Investing

After being a landlord for several years, I enjoy mobile home investing because it really allows me to have time for myself. Since I am no longer a landlord, I do not have to deal with tenant issues. No more toilets to fix, no more calls late at night. Since I'm dealing with people who have a homeowner mentality, these folks know they are responsible for taking care of their home (why wouldn't they?). They know they need to make payments on their home every month. If not, they know they will lose their home. It's a win/win situation for everyone.

These days, I can really take the time to enjoy life and do the things I want to do, not only the things I have to do—and this is really why I entered the real estate business: for financial freedom. When I was a landlord, I felt that I still had a job. Though there was income coming in, this income was not passive income—I still had to work for it.

In mobile home investing, my income is truly passive income—payments just keep coming in long after I've finished doing all the work. And if they stop, these home-owners know they will lose their home. Simple as that.

I have come to realize that it's much better to be the bank than the property owner. As a former landlord, I know now who always gets paid—the bank. When expenses go up, who still gets paid? The bank. When vacancies arise, who still gets paid? The bank. When evictions occur, who still gets paid? The bank. Is it better to be a property owner or the bank? I'll let you decide.

Personally, I made the decision years ago that it was better to be the bank, and that decision has paid off. Now I can enjoy true passive income through mobile home investing. And I can honestly say that mobile home investing has been my path to financial freedom.

We all have different paths in life. Sometimes the choices we make take us to new places, unknown places. With the unknown comes fear and uncertainty, but also with it comes possibilities. What isn't even imaginable in our wildest dreams becomes what is possible.

Maybe mobile home investing will be part of your dreams, maybe it will not. Whatever you choose, whatever you decide to do, I hope this book has helped you to see the possibilities.

Conclusion

Now that you have read this book, you have a general idea of how to get started in mobile home investing. I hope that sharing my own story has helped you to understand what it takes to become a mobile home investor, and to see that although our journeys are not always smooth, they can lead us to great places.

To be honest, this journey was not an easy one. It took work—hard work. I made many sacrifices. There were times when I just wanted to give up. But it was my passion and determination to succeed that kept me going. Without that, I would have never made it.

In writing this book, I hope to have shown you step by step what I did to get started in mobile home investing. I've shared with you the triumphs but also the obstacles and frustrations that I faced. It was the hurdles that were the toughest to overcome that taught me the most. I learned by doing and taking action. Sure, I made mistakes, but if I had not taken action then I would not be where I am today.

After reading this book, I urge you to take a look at your own goals and think about the kind of life you would like to live. My own decision to pursue mobile home investing stemmed out of my desire to live a life that would give me more time to do the things I wanted to do. It was this desire that really pushed me to keep going and to succeed no matter what obstacles I faced.

Look at this book as a starting point to get you thinking about your own personal journey in life. Think about where you want to be and what you want to do. Figure out your "why." What are you passionate about? What inspires you? If you figure out your "why" first, then the "how to" will eventually come together.

Once you figure out your "why," then you will be able to start mapping out your plan to get where you want to be. At first, it may seem overwhelming and your fears may settle in. Once you get started and get your plan together, though, it will not be as scary. With each step you take, you will be closer to reaching your goals. Reading this book is one of the first steps in your journey.

So go out into the world and write your own history. Choose your path and start your journey. As I have shared my story, I look forward to hearing yours!

Happy investing!

Rachel Hernandez
(aka "Mobile Home Gurl")
www.adventuresinmobilehomes.com

Acknowledgments

First, I would like to thank all of the many people who have visited and supported me and my website, *Adventures in Mobile Homes*. Thank you all so much for your comments and support. It was through the website and all the positive feedback I received that I was inspired to write this book. I feel both humbled and honored to continue to provide the information I have learned through my own experiences investing in mobile homes to you, the fans.

Second, I would like to thank all of my many mentors and teachers who have taken the time to teach and guide me through the years. It is individuals like you who truly want to see others succeed that really make this a better world for us all to live in. Without you, I would not be where I am today. By sharing my experiences and what I have learned, I hope to give back and teach others as you have given to me. Thank you.

Third, I would like to thank all of my fellow real estate blogger friends for all of your support and for your enthusiasm for *Adventures in Mobile Homes*. It is through you that I have come to realize it's better to surround myself with like-minded people. Thank you for taking the time to visit my website and share it with others.

Finally, I would like to thank the many individuals who have made this book possible. To my editor, Leila Kalmbach, who has spent countless hours helping me to focus on my prose and get this book in a publishable format. It has definitely been a very long and trying experience. I would also like to thank Cathi Stevenson for her wonderful book cover design. It has been a pleasure to work with her. Last but not least, I would like to thank Darlene Swanson for her great typesetting and layout for this book. Formatting and making a book easy to read is not an easy feat and is sometimes overlooked. I really appreciate your efforts and hard work, as you have all helped to make this book what it is today.

About the Author

Rachel Hernandez spent several years as a landlord before taking the leap to specializing in mobile home investing. Through a decade of experience in real estate investing, Rachel has learned about many different aspects of the real estate industry.

Rachel started out, like most real estate investors, investing in single family homes. In the beginning, she worked with several other investors, helping them to find deals. After awhile, she started doing deals herself. With the buy-and-hold mind-set of a landlord, Rachel found herself always working and was burned out from being a landlord. So she dove into the wacky world of mobile home investing and has not looked back since. To her, it's much more fun.

Rachel is the creator of *Adventures in Mobile Homes*, a blog dedicated to sharing her stories and adventures investing in mobile homes. Through the site, she aims to inspire and help others with what she has learned on her personal journey in mobile home investing.

Apart from her interest in real estate investing, Rachel has a background in both marketing and sales. As a former business-to-business sales executive for a Fortune 500 corporation, Rachel has extensive training in the area of sales and marketing. In addition, she has also worked in both the film and television industries in a business theatrical marketing and public relations capacity, respectively.

In her spare time, Rachel enjoys writing, reading, traveling and, especially, watching a good movie. Her passions for business, writing, entertaining and film stem from her childhood and are still burning strong. In everything she does, she aims to create the kind of life where she can do the things she wants to do, not only the things she has to do.

Rachel, also known as Mobile Home Gurl, can be contacted through her blog, *Adventures in Mobile Homes* (http://www.adventuresinmobilehomes.com), where she writes and produces videos regularly about her adventures investing in mobile homes. Rachel Hernandez has one investing strategy: K.I.S.—Keep It Simple.

For more information about mobile home investing, visit http://www.adventuresinmobilehomes.com.

Appendix 1

Checklists, Scripts and Sample Documents

Setting up Your Office Checklist

Here is a sample checklist to help you get started in setting up your office. These are just a few suggestions. Remember, cater your business to your own personality and style of doing things.

- Basic computer

- Basic printer

- Cell phone
    - → Google Voice number
      (http://www.google.com/voice)

- Mailing address (e.g., P.O. box, professional mailing address, etc.)

- Dedicated email address

- Dedicated fax number (recommended: Jfax –
  http://www.jfax.com)

- Basic office supplies
  - ❏ White printer paper
  - ❏ Notebook (for taking notes, logging seller/buyer calls, etc.)
  - ❏ Pens
  - ❏ Paper clips
  - ❏ Highlighters
  - ❏ Black markers
  - ❏ Staple gun (if using signs)
  - ❏ Thumbtacks (for posting up flyers)
  - ❏ Packing tape (for posting up flyers)
  - ❏ Scissors
- Financial calculator (recommended: HP 10BII)
- Marketing materials (recommend: Vista Print – http://www.vistaprint.com)
  - ❏ Business cards
  - ❏ Flyers
  - ❏ Signs
  - ❏ Door hangers
- Digital camera
- Flashlight
- Other items
  - ❏ Voice recorder
  - ❏ Basic toolbox

Build Your Team Checklist

This is a sample checklist to help you get started in building your team. These are just a few suggestions. Remember, cater your business to your own personality and style of doing things.

- Personal support network
  - ❏ Friends
  - ❏ Spouse
  - ❏ Family members
  - ❏ Other investors

- Mentors
  - ❏ Local
  - ❏ Regional
  - ❏ National

- Park managers

- Mobile home dealerships

- Contractors
  - ❏ Handyman
  - ❏ Electrician
  - ❏ Plumber
  - ❏ Heating and air-conditioning specialist
  - ❏ Landscaper
  - ❏ Flooring specialist
  - ❏ Painter
    - → Interior
    - → Exterior
  - ❏ Carpenter

- Cleaning crew

- Carpet cleaners

- Mobile home movers

- Local government housing authority

- Real estate agents

- Other real estate investors
  - ❏ Buyers (rehabbers, landlords, etc.)
  - ❏ Private lenders
  - ❏ Potential partners

- Insurance agent

Mobile Home Seller Call Lead Sheet

Date: _____

How did you hear about me? _____

_____

Name_____

Phone number _____

Address_____

Park name _____ Lot # _____

Is the home on land? _____

How much is the lot/land rent? _____

Does the home need to be moved? _____

Year of home _____ Size of home _____

Make and model of home _____

Number of bedrooms _____ Number of bathrooms _____

How long on the market? _____

Condition of home _____

Does home need repair work?   ❏ Y   or   ❏ N

If so, what needs work? _____

_____

_____

_____

What appliances are staying with the home?_____

_____

Is the home electric, gas or both? _____

Do you own the home? Who is on the title? _____

_____

How long have you been living in the home? _____

Do you have pets?   ❏ Y   or   ❏ N

Is the home vacant?   ❏ Y   or   ❏ N

Are the taxes paid?   ❏ Y   or   ❏ N

How much are the taxes every year? _____

Is there insurance on the home?   ❏ Y   or   ❏ N

Monthly insurance payment: _____

When do you need to sell by? _____

Why are you selling? _____

What is your asking price? _____

Are you flexible on the price? _____

Are you willing to finance?   ❏ Y   or   ❏ N

What is your best cash price? _____

Is there anything else you can tell me about the home? _____

_____

_____

_____

_____

_____

What is the best day and time to see the home? _____

_____

_____

Mobile Home Buyer Lead Sheet

Date: _____

How did you hear about the home? _____

Name _____

Phone number _____

How many people? _____

Have you driven by the home? _____

Are you familiar with the park and/or surrounding area? ❏ Y or ❏ N

How long have you lived in the area? _____

Where do you currently live? _____

How long have you been looking? _____

When are you looking to move? _____

Are you in a lease? ❏ Y   or   ❏ N

If yes, when does it end? _____

How much can you afford per month? _____

How much can you put down? _____

Do you have pets? ❏ Y   or   ❏ N

If so, what kind and how large? _____

_____

_____

Note: If the potential buyer has not driven by the home yet, tell him or her to drive by the home and check out the park and/or surrounding area. If after driving by the home he or she is still interested, the buyer can call you again to set up a time to view the home. Be sure to know the rules and regulations of the parks you are doing business in beforehand.

Learn Your Market Worksheet
(Park/Land/Dealer)

Date: _____

Park name _____

Park manager _____

Park address _____

Park phone number _____

Office hours _____

Type of park: ❏ Low-end

❏ Middle-of-the-road

❏ High-end

Number of lots _____

Lot rent amount _____

Single wide spaces _____

Double wide spaces _____

Deposit amount _____

Application fee _____

Application process _____

Restrictions? _____

Dogs allowed? ❏ Y or ❏ N

Pet restrictions? _____

Pet deposit _____

Amenities in park _____

Type of park: _____ Family style

_____ 55+ community

_____ Renters

Other _____

Percentage of homeowners versus renters _____

Average age of homes in park _____

Average size of homes in park _____

Average wholesale value _____

Average retail value _____

Average owner finance value _____

Average monthly payment (lot rent included) _____

Average down payment _____

Average holding time _____

What types of homes are people looking for? (e.g., 3 bedrooms, 2 bedrooms, larger, smaller, etc.): _____

_____

_____

Amenities near park (e.g., grocery, gas station, etc.): _____

_____

_____

Additional info _____

_____

_____

Goal and Exit Strategy Worksheet

Short-Term Goals

What are my short-term goals? _____

_____

_____

_____

_____

_____

_____

_____

_____

_____

Examples: Time frame to learn the market?

I'd like to do my first deal in X months.

How much do I want to spend on my first deal?

How much cash flow do I want from my first deal?

How much cash do I need to build up? In how much time?

How will I build up cash?

Am I ready to buy and hold?

What is my short-term exit strategy? _____

_____

_____

_____

_____

Long-Term Goals

What are my long-term goals? _____

_____

_____

_____

_____

_____

_____

_____

_____

_____

_____

Examples: What is my "why"? What is my passion?

How many deals do I want to have all together? In how much time?

What am I looking to achieve?

What kind of lifestyle do I imagine myself living?

Mobile Home Inspection Checklist

This is a sample checklist to help you with your mobile home inspections. These are just a few suggestions. Some homes may have other areas that need to be inspected.

Interior

- Living room
  - ❏ Ceiling
  - ❏ Walls
  - ❏ Windows
  - ❏ Floor
  - ❏ Any defects?

- Kitchen and dining area
  - ❏ Ceiling
  - ❏ Walls
  - ❏ Windows
  - ❏ Floor
  - ❏ Sink
  - ❏ Appliances working?
  - ❏ Any defects?

- Hallway
  - ❏ Ceiling
  - ❏ Walls

- ❏ Floor
- ❏ Heating and air conditioning working?
- ❏ Any defects?

- Number of bedrooms
  - ❏ Ceiling
  - ❏ Walls
  - ❏ Floor
  - ❏ Closets
  - ❏ Windows
  - ❏ Any defects?

- Number of bathrooms
  - ❏ Ceiling
  - ❏ Walls
  - ❏ Floors
  - ❏ Windows
  - ❏ Sink
  - ❏ Shower/tub
  - ❏ Any defects?

Exterior

- ❏ Siding (aluminum/masonite/wood)
- ❏ Skirting
- ❏ Front porch and deck
- ❏ Back porch stairs

- ❏ Roof
- ❏ Landscaping and trees
- ❏ Exterior windows
- ❏ Gutters
- ❏ Label and/or serial number (back of home)
- ❏ Painting needed?
- ❏ Carport?
- ❏ Parking spaces?
- ❏ Outdoor shed?
- ❏ Any defects?

- • What is staying/not staying with the home?
  - ❏ Appliances
    - → Refrigerator
    - → Washer and dryer
    - → Stove
  - ❏ Heating and air conditioning
  - ❏ Front porch and deck
  - ❏ Back porch and stairs
  - ❏ Carport
  - ❏ Outdoor shed
  - ❏ Miscellaneous
    - → Curtains
    - → Mini blinds
    - → Ceiling fans
    - → Anything else?

- ❏ What are the major issues with the home?
- ❏ What items need work?
  - → Approximately how much will it cost to fix up?
  - → How long will it take to fix up?
- ❏ Were you able to check all of the main systems in the home?
- ❏ Was everything working properly?
- ❏ What issues did you see?
- ❏ Is the seller willing to fix any defects? Or are they selling "as-is"?
- ❏ Is the home habitable?
- ❏ Anything else?

Mobile Home Cleaning Checklist

This is a sample checklist to help you with your mobile home cleanings. These are just a few suggestions.

Interior

- Living room
  - ❏ Walls
    - → Dirty or clean?
    - → Do they need to be painted?
  - ❏ Windows
    - → Dirty or clean?
    - → How about the windowsills?
  - ❏ Floor
    - → Dirty or clean?
    - → Are there any soft spots?
- Kitchen
  - ❏ Walls and cabinets
    - → Dirty or clean?
    - → Do they need to be painted?
  - ❏ Appliances
    - → Stove
    - → Refrigerator
  - ❏ Windows
    - → Dirty or clean?

→ How about the windowsills?

❏ Floor

→ Dirty or clean?

→ Are there any soft spots?

- Bathrooms

  ❏ Walls and cabinets

  ❏ Mirror (if applicable)

  ❏ Toilet

  ❏ Shower/tub

  ❏ Floor

- Bedrooms

  ❏ Walls and doors

  ❏ Floor

  ❏ Windows

- Exterior

  ❏ Front door

  → Dirty or clean?

  → Does it need to be painted?

  ❏ Front porch and deck

  → Dirty or clean?

  → Does it need to be painted?

  ❏ Siding

  → Dirty or clean?

  → Does it need to be painted?

❏ Skirting

  → Is it in place?

❏ Landscaping

  → Any overgrown grass, bushes or trees?

  → Leaves or debris?

  → Does the yard look clean?

SAMPLE BILL OF SALE

For and in consideration of _____ dollars

($_____) and other good and valuable consideration, the

receipt of which is hereby acknowledged, _____

and _____ hereby sell(s) to

_____ the property as described as follows:

Description:

a.   Size: _____ x _____ foot mobile home

b.   Trade name: 19_____

Model _____

c.   Identification number: _____

_____

d.   Location: Lot _____, _____

Mobile Home Park

e.   Personal property: central air conditioning unit (SN

_____); refrigerator (SN_____);

and stove (SN _____)

The Seller covenants that he/she is the lawful owner of such property
and that it is free from all encumbrances and certifies no liens exist on
the home and that park lot rent is current. Seller certifies that he/she
has the right to sell the same as the aforesaid and that he/she will warrant and defend the same against the lawful claims and demands of all

persons. Seller warrants that all appliances, plumbing, air-conditioning and heating units are in working order at the time of sale.

Seller agrees to possession date of _____ to Buyer. Seller agrees to remove all personal contents inside home and trash and debris from premises. Upon possession, Seller will hand over all keys to home to Buyer.

Signed at _____, _____, this ____ day of _____, 20 ____.

_____ Seller	_____ Buyer
_____ (Print)	_____ (Print)
Sworn and subscribed before me	Sworn and subscribed before me
this ____ day of _____, 20____	this ____ day of _____, 20____
_____ Signature of notary	_____ Signature of notary
SEAL	SEAL
_____ Seller	_____ Buyer
_____ (Print)	_____ (Print)
Sworn and subscribed before me	Sworn and subscribed before me
this ____ day of _____, 20____	this ____ day of _____, 20____
_____ Signature of notary	_____ Signature of notary
SEAL	SEAL

Sample Notice (for Nonpayment)

ABC Company

3310 Apple View Court, Suite 32

Bellevue, WA 98004

425-678-5777

PAST DUE NOTICE

January 6, 2010

To: Joe and Sue Buyer

Address: 123 Lemon Lane, Lot 10 Bellevue, WA 98004

Payment Period:	January 1, 2010
Amount Due:	$350.00
Late Charges Due:	$25.00
Total Due:	$375.00

Your account is past due. We have not received the above payment for your account.

Please contact us to make payment arrangements on your account. Your prompt response will be appreciated. Failure to pay past due amounts will result in further action and additional costs to bring your account current.

Steve Smith

Manager

ABC Company

Sample Closing Document Checklist, Sellers

Many of these forms can be found in other mobile home investing books. Please refer to the "Recommended Reading" section for a list of reference books.

- Mobile home purchase agreement

- Bill of sale (see sample included here)

- Local housing authority paperwork for title transfer

- Fee for title transfer to local housing authority

- Taxes paid up to local taxing authority

- Receipt book

Sample Closing Document Checklist, Buyers

Similar forms can be found in other mobile home investing books. Please refer to the "Recommended Reading" section for a list of reference books.

- Credit application

- Mobile home sales agreement

- Promissory note

- Lease with purchase option agreement (if any)

- Home warranty (if any)

- Smoke detector verification

- Receipt book

Appendix 2

Recommended Resources

Mobile Home Investing Books

Deals on Wheels by Lonnie Scruggs

Comprehensive book on buying, selling and financing used mobile homes. The book that started it all!

Making Money with Mobile Homes by Lonnie Scruggs

Considered the next important book after *Deals on Wheels*. More stories and details on buying, selling and financing used mobile homes.

Mobile Home Wealth by Zalman Velvel

In-depth book about buying, selling and renting mobile homes.

Making Money through Mobile Home Investing by Jerry Hoganson

Book answering questions on the business of mobile home investing.

Mobile Home Repair Books

The Manual for Manufactured/Mobile Home Repair and Upgrade by Mark N. Bower

Covering the ins and outs of "do it yourself" mobile home repairs and upgrades.

Your Mobile Home: Energy and Repair Guide for Manufactured Housing by John T. Krigger

Guidebook answering questions about mobile and manufactured homes. Includes drawings, photos, charts and graphs.

Personal Finance Books

Rich Dad, Poor Dad by Robert Kiyosaki

Teaches about the concept of "cash flow" and how it can be applied in real life.

The Richest Man in Babylon by George S. Clawson

Stories about business and finance.

The Automatic Millionaire by David Bach

Personal financial planning by automating contributions to retirement and investment vehicles.

Marketing and Sales Books

Sales Dogs by Blair Singer

Teaches about the different breeds of salespeople to improve sales savviness.

Little Red Book of Selling by Jeffrey Gitomer

Teaches the principles of sales greatness to improve sales ability.

Permission Marketing by Seth Godin

Focusing on the art of permission marketing by teaching how to turn strangers into friends and friends into customers.

The One Minute Sales Person by Spencer Johnson

Insightful book on how to be a great salesperson.

Influence by Robert Cialdini

In-depth look at the power of influence and how it can be used in everyday life.

Secrets of Power Persuasion by Roger Dawson

Teaching the art of persuasion to help you achieve your personal and professional goals.

Websites

BiggerPockets – http://www.biggerpockets.com
Community real estate investing forum with a mobile
home investing discussion group.

Lonnie Scruggs – http://www.LonnieScruggs.net
Articles, tips and information on how to make money
buying, selling and financing used mobile homes.

Mobile Home University –
http://www.mobilehomeuniversity.com
Mobile home investing community forum and
message board.

Mobile Home Repair – http://www.mobilehomerepair.com
Articles, tips and message board to help people
understand how to repair and maintain manufactured
homes.

REI Club – http://www.reiclub.com
Articles and tips on mobile home investing.

Business Resources

Gmail – http://www.gmail.com

Google Voice – http://www.google.com/voice

Jfax – http://www.jfax.com

Vista Print – http://www.vistaprint.com

For more recommended resources, visit the "Resources" section at http://www.adventuresinmobilehomes.com.

Made in the USA
Lexington, KY
17 June 2016